The LINE OF THE BALL

The LINE OF THE BALL

Leadership, Legacy, and Lifelong Lessons in Family, Business, and Sport

DR. BEH CHUN CHUAN

Forbes | Books

Published by Forbes Books, Charleston, South Carolina.
An imprint of Advantage Media Group.

Printed in China.

10 9 8 7 6 5 4 3 2 1

ISBN: 979-8-88750-734-7 (Hardcover)
ISBN: 979-8-88750-735-4 (eBook)

Library of Congress Control Number: 2025906555

Cover design by Matthew Morse.
Layout design by Ruthie Wood.

06-25-2025 11:47

Contents

Chevy Beh, first Asian to represent Tianjin World Snow Polo Championship, China

Preface

This memoir is dedicated to my late son, Dato' Chevy Beh, who inspired me to tell my story. Indeed, it was Chevy's encouragement that gave me the motivation and determination to complete this book.

Throughout his life, Chevy always strived to be better than me in all areas—whether in business or polo. If he felt he hadn't surpassed my achievements, he was disappointed in himself. He was constantly striving to overachieve.

Chevy and I spent a lot of time together, and we loved to travel with one another. He had a very special personality that made him uplifting to be around. Thanks to him, I saw many parts of the world I would not have discovered otherwise, as he introduced me to many new cultures and experiences, all of which were even more enjoyable when we explored them together.

Chevy was also a Forbes Healthcare contributor for Asia, and the idea for this book first entered my mind at the Forbes Healthcare Summit in New York City in 2012, following my interview for the Forbes podcast. After I shared my company, BP Healthcare Group's, business model, Forbes realized that it is unique in the way it integrates primary, secondary, and tertiary care, as well as the multitude of services we offer patients.

I was then encouraged to write a biography of my journey building BP Healthcare Group to share my healthcare business story. The book was started before the COVID-19 outbreak but was put on hold midway through the pandemic.

Since Chevy sadly passed away in 2022, I was remotivated to write the book in his memory, in honor of his unwavering passion and persuasion for me to share my journey with the rest of the world. I hope to demonstrate to people of all backgrounds and walks of life that through hard work, dedication, and kindness to others, it is possible to achieve success and happiness.

During the Forbes Healthcare Summit in 2023, I had the opportunity to speak with Mr. Steve Forbes to convey my wish to complete the book and publish it in memory of my late son. I am therefore eternally grateful for Steve's support in bringing this project to life so Chevy's legacy lives on.

The true driving force behind my success in all my endeavors is my love for my family. I would also like to express my heartfelt appreciation to my late mother, brothers, sisters, my wife, and my children—Lovy, Joevy, and Garvy—all of whom consistently champion me to pursue my dreams. They have been critical pillars in the pursuit of my tertiary education, leading me to become the first university graduate in my family. Throughout my business journey, their prayers and support have also given me added confidence to execute new business ventures with gusto.

It is their endless support that keeps me energized and motivated to keep going each and every day.

Three-generation family photo

Introduction

My life has changed more than I could ever have imagined since my humble beginnings. Born as the youngest of seven siblings, in the rural town of Bagan Serai, Malaysia, I have become one of the country's most successful business leaders, owning and running one of Malaysia's largest and most innovative healthcare groups. Yet I attribute much of my success today to the work ethic, survival skills, resilience of character, and independent problem-solving abilities I learned during my childhood.

When I was growing up during the baby boomer era, it was thought that tertiary education was a passport to a better quality of life because of access to more career opportunities. Graduates were in short supply in Malaysia because of the limited number of universities, courses, and entrance opportunities. This "good grades equals good career" equation overlooks essential skills needed for entrepreneurial success. I grew up learning from real-life, hands-on experience—being part of the Boy Scouts, helping my parents sell tropical fruits, and exploring nature rather than reading textbooks.

While academic achievement is important, it is only one piece of the puzzle. True success requires intuition, critical thinking, and creativity to develop new ideas and make them into reality, not just to "copy and paste" from others. Outstanding entrepreneurs must be able to monetize ideas through ingenuity, perseverance, strong leadership, and clear communication.

Early Business Lessons

Even from a very young age, my parents taught me the importance of turnaround time, and I learned that everything had to be done quickly in our business, as any delay with perishable tropical fruits was a financial loss to the family.

At this very early stage in my life, I did not need money to be happy. Indeed, I found the greatest happiness in simple pleasures, such as enjoying outdoor activities and playing sports. My parents empowered my siblings and me with the responsibility that whenever we needed pocket money, we could go to the petty cash drawer in our shop, and they trusted us to only take what we needed. They didn't check how much we took, and the petty cash drawer was never left empty, as we didn't need much to live on and were not greedy for money. This system worked, and if my parents noticed there was less money in the drawer than usual, they would ask us about it over dinner.

As I got older and moved to the city to study at secondary school, it was an eye-opening experience for me. I found out that everything you do for recreation in the city costs money. This was when I realized I could no longer pass my time without money by just enjoying nature alone; I was required to purchase everything I needed. I also began to be exposed to more successful people and a more aspirational lifestyle. For instance, I saw my peers being driven to school by chauffeurs in flashy cars, riding large motorcycles, and living in substantial bungalow houses.

This fueled my determination and ambition to improve my own circumstances, and I was prepared to study and work very hard to reach the level of economic success I aspired to, and that is what I did. I founded BP Healthcare Group in 1980, and at that time I could have never anticipated that what started as a relatively small-scale pathology testing laboratory would grow into a group offering primary, secondary, and tertiary healthcare services across Malaysia.

Many people question how, from such a modest start in life as the son of local fruit wholesalers, I have achieved this. When people say to my family and me, "You are so lucky," I reply, "Yes, we are lucky." But the reality is we have made ourselves lucky, and we've made a lot of sacrifices. We work hard to run a profitable business with the help of our excellent professional team.

When it comes to being lucky, I believe you make your own luck by building good karma and being blessed by God. Everyone has the power to put themselves in a position where they are likely to get more luck by working hard and being a good person. If you sit and wait for wealth to come to you without doing things righteously, it is unlikely to happen.

Maternal Wisdom and Values

I owe a lot to my late mother, with whom I spent a lot of time while growing up. While she was not rich financially, she passed on a wealth of character traits and life lessons to me, which have been invaluable in helping me reach where I am now. It is because of her caring and generous nature that I, too, make being nice to people a rule to live by. My mother taught me to be humble to everyone I meet, to always greet others first, and to show respect.

She also taught me the importance of giving back and having a benevolent heart. She told me not to do anything merely for money, as money should be secondary. If you live an honest life without cheating anyone, give to others, and show genuine care for others, you will reap the rewards. She believed in the power of good karma and the idea of past actions influencing present opportunities.

My mother used to tell my siblings and me a story about the god of prosperity. One day a gentleman encountered the god of prosperity in his dream, and the god said he would make the gentleman a rich man. So the man lived his life carefree, often getting drunk. Then one day the god of prosperity came to shower him with good fortune, but he was so drunk, he couldn't receive the blessing.

The moral of the story is to always prepare yourself to take on new opportunities when they arise. I am always ahead of other people—when a new opportunity presents itself, I am the first person to be able to grasp it. Moving with the times, adapting to the environment, and embracing and investing in new technology also give me an advantage, as I am constantly looking ahead to identify the next big thing in technology that will improve services for our customers. Some might call it luck, but I describe it as a combination of preparation meeting opportunity, foresight, and a lot of hard work.

Leadership Foundations

Being a Boy Scout is another influence that shaped much of my childhood and greatly influenced who I am today, as it trained me to be a leader, think outside the box, and learn survival skills. Following the Scout laws and promises gave me a sense of belonging and patriotism and inspired me to live a meaningful and honest life with integrity and respect for others.

At all times I practice the Boy Scouts' motto to "Be Prepared" by always thinking one step ahead. For example, I invest in property, equipment, digitalization, and training employees so we can activate resources to quickly scale up when required. Case in point: When COVID-19 hit, I already had the physical, digital, and human capital infrastructure to get testing services up and running overnight.

Lessons from Polo

Playing the fast-paced, adrenaline-fueled sport of polo has also influenced and challenged me in many ways. I often say that playing high-goal polo is one thousand times more complex than obtaining a Harvard MBA. The desire to win consumes players so completely that only death or bankruptcy will stop them from participating.

My family plays polo because we love the sport, and it has brought us together. Polo is a big part of our family life, and it has taught us all many values. It has encouraged us to be brave, quick in decision-making, and team players, and we get the benefit of the enjoyment of playing the sport while strengthening our family bond. Playing polo brings out the best and worst of your personality and capabilities. Hence playing together helps us learn more about each other so we can work together to utilize each other's strengths on and off the field.

The phrase "the line of the ball" is used in polo when you have hit the ball and an imaginary line is created between you and the ball, giving you the right-of-way to follow it. No other players can cross your line. Correct right-of-way is the most important rule in polo, and crossing the line of the ball is not only considered foul play but is also extremely dangerous and can be fatal because of the risk of a collision of horses and riders.

The line of the ball is also relevant in business, as it not only gives you a line of conduct to follow, but when you are the first to come up with a good idea or a new technology, the line of the ball also gives you a clear pathway to give it your best shot before anyone else. Of course, there will always be competitors following closely behind you to see if you miss the shot or to see if they can overtake you and get a hit of the ball after you, riding on your initial success. Or they might try to impede you altogether, just as the opposition in polo will try to "hook you"—another polo term used to describe a player hooking the mallet of the player taking the shot with their own mallet so the player is restrained from hitting the ball. In polo and business, you must keep pushing forward to claim your line and take your fair chance to hit the ball.

Ethics in Healthcare

The healthcare sector demands excellence and integrity, as the result is the patients, who should always get the best out of the services being provided. It is about following the line of the ball and playing fairly. You cannot compromise on quality and honesty in healthcare, and this is where BP Healthcare Group unwaveringly stands by its values. If you follow the line of the ball and conduct yourself and your business in an ethical way, you will reach your goals happier and with more good karma than those who take advantage of the innocent. Some corporations think they can, and will, do anything just to win a deal, but that is not sustainable in the long run. If you cheat, it will always come back to haunt you.

As long as I have followed the line of the ball, striving to provide the highest levels of quality, value, and turnaround times for my clients, I have no regrets in my business life. The only times I have felt disappointment are when I have respected and followed the line of the ball, but other shareholders or partners have crossed the line by cheating, causing a crash. I own BP Healthcare Group, so I can control how the business is run, and I ensure that the line of the ball guides my company in everything we do.

Perfecting the game of polo and competing at the highest level among professional players takes years of dedication and commitment. I have the utmost respect for the highest-rated, talented ten-goal polo players, such as Adolfo Cambiaso, who remains at the top of the sport because of sheer hard work and perseverance. I vividly remember around thirty years ago, I was in Argentina with Salvador Socas, the half brother of Adolfo Cambiaso. They were staying at Estancia La Martina, in the striking white house with the blue roof. Adolfo started riding early in the morning, then trained again in the afternoon, and played practice matches in the evening. He was essentially working three shifts each day, every day. That is why, after more than three decades, he is still one of the best polo players in the world and a true inspiration.

The Marathon of Success

Just as there are no shortcuts to becoming the world's number one in sport, there are no shortcuts to achieving business success, either, if your company is to have longevity. The aim of this book is not to give advice on how to "get rich quick," because the reality is that success is not a sprint race. It is a demanding marathon, where you're competing with the world's best—mentally and physically prepared individuals with drive, innovative ideas, and fierce determination to succeed.

By fostering a well-rounded approach and outlook from an early age, I believe we can prepare the next generation for the long-distance race of life. And I hope that by leading by example, living my life, and conducting my business by following and respecting the line of the ball, I will inspire current and future business leaders for years to come with my philosophy.

Beh family portrait

Chapter 1
SEEDS OF SUCCESS

From humble beginnings in rural Malaysia to life-changing experiences in the city, my early years laid the foundation for everything I would later achieve. Growing up as the youngest of seven children in a fruit-selling family taught me invaluable lessons about business, while my transition to city life and formal education opened my eyes to new possibilities. My journey from the simple streets of Bagan Serai to my educational transformation at Saint Michael's Institution reveals how childhood adventures, family values, and academic growth shaped my path to success.

Foundations in Family Business

My ancestors arrived in Malaysia after hardship and political unrest between the Communist Party and the National Kuomintang in China forced them to flee from the country in the late 1800s. To avoid poverty, starvation, and fear during that era, they settled in Malaysia, while others settled in other parts of Southeast Asia. At first, the conditions they faced in Malaysia were not much better than those they had left in China, but they left knowing they were going to a country with an abundance of untapped economic potential. Despite facing extreme austerity, they were frugal and able to save the little money and commodities they had, such as lard and bicycles, to send back to family who had stayed in their home village in China.

My childhood could be described as somewhat unconventional. I was born in a small town named Bagan Serai in the state of Perak, Malaysia, an area well known for its rice paddy fields, rubber, and palm oil plantations. As the youngest of seven siblings, I was the baby of my family. Back in those days, in the baby boomer period in the late 1950s, mine was considered a small family! The average number of children in a family was ten, and my aunt was one of seventeen siblings.

Because of Bagan Serai's rural location—around one hour drive north of the city of Ipoh, the capital of Perak state, and three hundred kilometers north of Kuala Lumpur—it was relatively underdeveloped, with farming and fishing being the main economic activities. However, despite it being quite rough around the edges, I enjoyed my childhood during the first fifteen years of my life, and it was there that I laid the foundations of many lessons and values I still strongly believe in today.

Along with my parents and my six siblings, we all lived together in a typical house on a commercial street lined with shop fronts, where people ran their businesses on the ground floor and lived in the rooms above—a common concept in Southeast Asia. Ours was a basic yet functional shop house, made of pre–World War II concrete on the ground level, with a wooden upper level. We lived upstairs in three rooms, while the business was run downstairs. We had a good tap water supply, but our sewage system was outdated, as it was collected daily in buckets.

My parents ran a fresh tropical fruit wholesale business, which was started by my father. Wholesale fruit was something he seemed to have a natural aptitude for. The business was our life, as everyone in the family had to work. We were not a particularly "poor" family in our town, but we were certainly living hand to mouth, and cash flow was always very tight.

My mother supported my father a lot with the financial and administrative side of the business, as my father's main skill set was manual labor. He provided the brawn, whereas my mom provided the brains. Indeed, my dad was just a small-time businessman, and while he never aspired to grow the business or make it any bigger than it was, I always admired him for his honest way of living and running the business, even though he didn't make much of a margin.

My dad was always so thoughtful about his customers, and he never cheated anyone. He was a shy, caring, and loving man with a very kind nature, but he earned very little money. As he wasn't educated, he was fearful of what he didn't know, and his business territory was very limited. However, because he never had a bank loan, he never had a stressful life. He didn't have to worry about bankruptcy or bank mortgage repayments. He lived a simple life, didn't demand much, and was content. There is nothing wrong with living like this, but I have the mindset of wanting to improve every day, and I never stop looking for the next thing to conquer and achieve. I learned the skills of preservation and taking care of customers from my father, prioritizing their needs over making money, but I had bigger aspirations.

It was my mother who raised the capital for the business during fruit season. My mom was exceptionally smart and credible, and she used "tontine" microcredit to generate funds. My dad was in charge of buying and selling, while my mom took charge of financial management. She was the dominant person in their relationship, but I always had a lot of respect for both of my parents.

Growing up around the fresh fruit wholesale business, I learned the key lesson that turnaround time is paramount. Everything had to be done quickly, as every delay was a loss to the family. Tropical fruit is especially perishable compared with temperate fruits, and if kept for more than one or two days, it spoils and becomes worthless. So even as the youngest child in my family, I contributed manpower to help move the fruit, and I developed a resourceful instinct for problem-solving and overcoming challenges, which would help with my business sensibilities later in life.

My siblings and I would often go to the market, and if we had to go to another town, we would jump into a government lorry, kind of like an old-school Uber. We would pay a nominal fee for the driver to take us there and drop us off with our baskets of fruit. On our return journey, we couldn't bring anything back apart from the weighing machine and cash in hand. We even sold the fruit baskets and packaging before the end of the day so we could catch a bus or hitch a ride from a "pirate" taxi after having a meal at the market. If we didn't sell them, they would be a burden to lug back with us.

Whenever we did have any produce left on market days, we would sell everything very cheaply to clear the stock and bring back at least some money. When we got home, my father often used to say, "You've sold it so cheap—no wonder you've sold it all!"

But while we sometimes got into a bit of trouble if we didn't sell all the produce, working with my parents never caused any problems for my siblings and me, as we all tried our best to serve our parents. We were smart enough not to make mistakes, and we generally always sold all the fruit before it perished. This understanding about turnaround time all comes back to a focus on execution and timing, which is crucial for the way I run BP Healthcare Group today.

Nature as a Classroom

The cost of living was generally cheap when I was growing up. For example, a coffee was maybe the equivalent of five cents in Malaysian ringgit. But one of the most important lessons I learned from a young age is that I didn't need money to enjoy life. When you grow up surrounded by nature, as I did, you're blessed with many different activities on your doorstep to occupy your time—from the river to the mountains and the jungle. As a child, there are hours of endless games awaiting you: playing hide-and-seek; climbing trees; building tents; watching and catching birds; fishing; keeping dogs, chickens, ducks, and geese; or swimming in waterfalls, ponds, and lakes.

The journey walking from my house to school was a few miles across the countryside. On my first day of school, my brother took me on a tricycle, and that was the first and only time he did. After that, he told me he was too busy, and from that day onward, my independent life began. From the second day of primary school, I had to walk there myself, regardless of whether it was in heavy rain or intense heat. Only in the last few years of primary school did I upgrade to cycling, but I never had the option of going by car.

I was a very independent child, as my parents were always busy working and didn't have time to give my six siblings and me a lot of attention, so we had to find our own ways of making our lives interesting. When we weren't helping our parents sell fruit or exploring nature, we would be playing all kinds of sports, from badminton to football and hockey. I learned how to play many sports when I was a child, and while I wasn't especially good at any one of them, it was the transferable skills I learned—sportsmanship, leadership, resilience, and teamwork—that taught me how to win in life.

In volleyball I was a reserve player, and my team won the state provincial championship. Despite sitting out and watching the game as a reserve player, leading up to the match, I still turned up and trained with the rest of the team, so I also got rewarded with a trophy at the end. That was a lesson in how staying committed and supporting my team, even if I was not picked for the game, paid off.

Another experience that brought me a lot of fun and enjoyment as a child was being in the Boy Scouts, an organization now internationally headquartered in Malaysia. I am still involved today as a committee member of the National Council and as a trustee. I joined the Boy Scouts as a Cub in Bagan Serai when I was ten years old, and I quickly became a Cub leader. I always encourage children and young people to join the Boy Scouts, because not only was it a lot of fun and took me on many adventures, but it also taught me invaluable survival skills and life lessons, in addition to confidence, problem-solving abilities, a sense of belonging, and an understanding of how to live and work in harmony with nature.

Joining the Boy Scout Movement allowed me the freedom to enjoy outdoor activities with other Scouts, without my family worrying about me too much. My mom and my nanny even used to make up ghost stories to scare me from exploring in the jungle and swimming in the rivers on my own. The Boy Scouts also taught me many core values I hold close and how to be a leader.

The two Scout Laws and ten Promises, which you make when you become a Scout, are important for inspiring children to be more patriotic and for enabling them to live meaningful and honest lives with integrity. I strongly believe in the Scout Law, which says that a Scout should be trustworthy, loyal, friendly, and considerate; have courage in all difficulties; make good use of time; be careful with possessions and property; and have self-respect and respect for others.

The Scout Promise varies slightly for different age groups, but the fundamental message is to always do your best, be kind and helpful, love God and show love to other people, respect the laws of the land, set a good example, and make a positive contribution to society. The Boy Scouts also taught me that you must do at least one good deed every day, and that has helped me create good karma.

In the Scouts I found out I was a natural leader. As young as ten years old, I would take groups of my fellow Cubs on camping trips and outdoor activities as a Cub leader. In 1972, at the age of sixteen, I became a King's Scout, the highest rank in Scouting, which is usually only achieved by those over eighteen. King's Scouts are also examiners, so I would examine junior Scouts when they did tests to earn their proficiency badges. Generally, I didn't fail anyone, as I never wanted to make life difficult for anyone else. Instead, if someone did not yet have the necessary skills or knowledge, I would rather try to teach them and help them learn so they could gain the ability to pass. To me, this is a much more constructive way of helping people progress and improve.

It never crossed my mind to fail someone out of jealousy because I didn't want someone else to have the same success as I had. I learned from my mother never to be jealous or selfish, and I never feared or felt threatened by people who had the same standard or who were better than me. Today it actually brings me joy to teach my staff and see them grow and develop, as this then helps them teach others, allowing my office to run by itself. Rather than withholding knowledge and skills for myself, I have always liked to pass on as much of my expertise as possible to my staff, as you need to empower your workforce to keep growing your business and take it to the next level. Giving my staff independence and responsibility also frees me up to seek new opportunities to expand my businesses outside of BP Healthcare Group.

I may have had a leadership role in the Scouts, but I was also involved in mischief and some fooling around. Our school often hosted gatherings around a campfire where both Boy Scouts and Girl Guides would come together from different schools, and I was always in charge of organizing the entertainment. Usually this would involve me and some of the other Boy Scouts coming up with an impromptu drama sketch and performing it in front of everyone.

When I say sketch, it was always an unscripted show that we made up on the spot, like a stand-up comedy show, but we never planned it out. Every time we held these gatherings or went to another school and there was talk of a performance, everyone would always say, "Ask Beh!" and I would mastermind an idea and come up with some funny jokes. There were a few of my friends who would also perform with me, so we were a trio, and I would direct us.

Looking back, I am not even sure if my jokes were particularly funny, but every time I performed, everyone seemed to laugh a lot. Perhaps they weren't even laughing at the content of the jokes, but they just thought I was a bit of a clown. Either way, the sketches were definitely entertaining for everyone, and performing like this taught me not to be shy or to take myself too seriously. When I think about why our trio was so popular and why we always got asked to put on shows, it was our ability to make people laugh that made us very likable. I always remind myself that if ever I failed in my business endeavors, my backup career plan could be stand-up comedy.

While leading a group of Scouts once, I remember a group of us went swimming in an irrigation canal that was out of bounds, as the water there was meant for drinking. We didn't realize swimming there was prohibited; we thought it was only for irrigating the surrounding paddy fields. Inspectors would pass by the canal to forbid anyone from swimming. When the smarter kids in the group, including me, saw them from afar, we quickly picked up our clothes and shoes and ran away. Even from this young age, you could tell which of us were the vigilant kids.

The less observant members of the group got caught, and all their clothes were taken by the inspectors straight to the headmaster. So they had to go to the headmaster with only banana leaves to hide their decency! I also had to go to the headmaster, but I had my clothes on at least. It was hilarious. Even today, when I see those friends, they still blame me, as I was their leader. But I just say to them that they were not astute enough; they should have run away sooner when they first sensed a threat. They were too preoccupied enjoying themselves playing in the water and not aware of the dangers.

My sense of adventure has stayed with me into adulthood. When I visited Mendoza, between Chile and Argentina, there was a flagpole I climbed. Everyone around me, including the Argentine tour guide and my son, told me I was crazy to attempt it, because it was dangerous. But I spent so much of my childhood climbing trees to catch birds, I know how to climb. I also find it fun to do nightclub pole dancing to show my children that I am crazier than them and to prove I am still healthy and strong at sixty-eight years old, with six-pack abs.

It is practical skills and fearlessness that make me a good businessman. Put me in any difficult situation and I can wriggle out of it. It is also about having the confidence and courage to take calculated risks. Give me any company and I can identify and solve the problems, as I know how to think out of the box to find where the weaknesses are and how to overcome them. I am always passionate; I pursue things wholeheartedly, and I never give up.

Academic Awakening

Instead of going to kindergarten, I went straight to primary school at the age of seven. Education was not a big focus for me during my years in primary and lower secondary school. My report cards were filled with negative comments marked in red ink. My parents never saw them, though. They couldn't afford an education for themselves, and they never checked in on how I was doing at school or asked how my exams had gone. They were too busy working, so I had the freedom to do whatever I wanted at school. To my parents, it was more important that I learned through real-life experience, such as helping to trade fruit in our family business from a young age. I forged my parents' Chinese signatures on all my report cards through college, fooling my teachers each time.

I didn't even know what subjects we were learning at school most of the time, and when we had tests and exams, I wasn't aware, so I never revised for them. When our usual teacher was away, the substitute teacher who was covering the class would always instruct the class monitor to write down the names of unruly pupils, and my name was almost always guaranteed to be at the top of the list. I was more cheeky and playful than badly behaved, but I was pretty disruptive, with a lot of tricks up my sleeve. That is why I always said if I needed a backup plan in life, I could be a stand-up comedian.

But while I wasn't very engaged in my early education, I did enjoy geography, because my form teacher, Peter Santhosam, who was also my geography teacher and school scoutmaster, made the subject interesting. Surprisingly I easily achieved an A grade in this subject. Geography helped me carry over some learning patience and confidence to other classes and was a turning point for my education, as I learned I had a photographic memory and could excel in any subject if I devoted time to it.

I also used to enjoy doing art at school and creating watercolor paintings, as I had an inherent ability for art, as did all my siblings, especially my sister Mah Ah Ching, who is a nationally renowned artist. I would love to have time to revisit my passion for art these days in my adult life, as it is very therapeutic, but unfortunately, because of my demanding 24/7 work schedule, I am currently unable to find any time to pursue artistic endeavors.

I was generally unguided with minimal supervision growing up, and in my opinion this modern generation of children is overprotected by their parents, so they cannot think for themselves when they reach young adulthood.

Reflections on Modern Learning

These days, parents seem to have a lot of time to spend giving their children all the materials and resources they think they need. Tiny children get sent to preschool when they are only two or three years old, before starting primary school at age seven. And during their school years, they have the same information repeated and hammered into them over and over again. It is no wonder children get bored, as their brains are filled up with dry facts and information from textbooks, which is a very passive way of learning.

In our modern world, the direction in which things are moving is that many children don't even read from textbooks now; they consume everything digitally. Often in restaurants I see families with children, where the parents have given the kids a tablet or mobile phone at the dinner table. Going out to a restaurant should be family bonding time, but these days everyone at the table has their own gadgets, which they are concentrating on. The children don't give the parents any trouble because they are transfixed by the screen. While children are becoming increasingly tech savvy, they are inevitably losing human social skills.

This is why, even with so much information available online, I believe children should still go to school to engage in social interaction in the classroom and in the playground, as learning how to interact with other people is incredibly important for developing their social and emotional intelligence.

This is where artificial intelligence (AI) can be very corruptive, particularly for young people, because a lot of data can be gained from their online habits, creating an echo chamber where they can be brainwashed and influenced into believing things they consume online. On the contrary, people who live by active learning and real-life skills think differently from the majority, as everything is a discovery to them, and they are curious and question what they are seeing or being told to believe. Most people have already been influenced by digital mass communication, especially those who indulge in too much time online, on social media, or watching a lot of TV; therefore their minds are already programmed in the same way as everyone else's.

Those who have been brought up in nature or who have had to work from an early age exploring for themselves have much more inquisitive and creative minds, which they can apply in different real-life situations, not just theoretical skills for sitting school exams. Unfortunately we are in an age of passive learning and a "copy and paste" culture, where memorizing extracts of text and churning it out again seems to be the formula for passing exams.

The Value of Active Learning

I suggest we think about careers or entrepreneurial success as a marathon, not a sprint race. Here, rote memorization alone won't suffice, and while a disciplined student with good study habits can excel in a copy-and-paste school or university environment, the real world demands much more. Indeed, this is why young generations, conditioned for academic sprints, struggle when they encounter the marathons of careers and entrepreneurship. They lack the creativity and resilience to navigate constant challenges and setbacks.

If you discover through nature, you become more open minded, and you can think of unique ideas. Take most billionaires—chances are, they did not come from Harvard or Oxford University. They are often from the school of hard knocks with formidable exposures and experiences in life that stimulate and activate their mental and physical faculties to give them what it takes to be successful, despite the odds being against them.

Elon Musk, for example, did not have an easy journey to success. He grew up in South Africa, and he was bullied growing up, which gave him resilience and a survival instinct. It also wasn't easy for him to move to America, as it's difficult for South Africans to get green cards, so he had to go via Canada, which is complex and time consuming. In comparison to someone who has more security and predictability in their life, he faced challenges, which are sure to have contributed to his extraordinary accomplishments. A predictable life means a predictable mind and results in a predictable outcome.

If I ran a school, I would not insist on children taking exams. Instead of regurgitating memorized answers under test conditions, I believe it is more important for children to be genuinely interested in a subject and apply their understanding in a real-world context.

However, these days it is worrying how kids and adults can go to tools such as ChatGPT, Google, and Gemini to copy and paste answers without understanding or absorbing the information.

I personally believe parents should move beyond the singular focus of pushing their children for academic achievement. It is crucial for children to have a balanced approach to education, one that includes spending time in nature, developing practical life skills, and fostering resilience, along with what they learn in the classroom. Equipping young people with these skills alongside academic excellence will empower them to handle the everyday pressures they'll face in the grown-up world and in any career they choose to pursue. It is also important to stress that academic success is an indicator of learning potential, not a guaranteed path to immediate career victory.

Learning from Life's Shadows

While I discovered the value of independence and the freedom of active learning, I appreciate this style of learning may be not effective for every child, especially those who, with a lack of parental guidance and supervision, may be led astray by negative influences. It is easier to learn from bad influences than good values, but I consider myself lucky that, even though I was exposed to good and bad growing up, I never fell in with the wrong crowd.

It is not that I was particularly focused at a young age; I was actually a very happy-go-lucky person, but I managed to stay on the right path, which enabled me to have the freedom to explore and evolve. I never got in trouble with my parents, and generally my parents never had any problems with any of my siblings, apart from my eldest brother. As we lived in a small town, when teenagers and young adults had too much free time, they would gamble, and my eldest brother fell into that trap.

Unfortunately, we could not avoid exposure to gambling growing up. Alongside my parents' fruit wholesale business, there was a darker side to how my mother balanced the books and made an income. During this dark era, there was a big flood, resulting in the destruction of fruit trees; hence we had to look for other ways to make a living.

In the back portion of our shop in Bagan Serai, we operated a gambling den. When customers would come in, it was my job to look at people and filter if they were gamblers or policemen. Indeed, when I was around fourteen years old, my side hustle was working in the gambling den operated by a local syndicate, which my mother became involved in, acting like a surveillance camera essentially. As the youngest child, I was the only one left to work and help my mom in Bagan Serai.

My mom was convinced by friends, and her argument for running the gambling den was that she needed more money for our family, but it was one way in which her good karma was destroyed. She was an incredibly kind and generous person, but no one is perfect when faced with dire financial circumstances.

From working in the gambling den, I learned there was a lot of cheating in this world. Even back then, over fifty years ago, there were magnets in the dice, so it wasn't fair play. In the end the gamblers would usually lose money, but my mom didn't really make much money from it, either, as she also had to pay the police to turn a blind eye to what was going on. Retrospectively we realized our past mistakes and how destructive it was for many families, who sold their properties and paddy fields and went bankrupt because of gambling.

At the time I was not fully aware of the implications of gambling, but looking back, I see how corrupt it was and how greed can overtake your senses. That is why I am very against gambling and have never gambled myself because of the repercussions I saw in the gambling den and how it negatively affected my eldest brother.

I believe God has always blessed me, so I don't need to be greedy and earn any more money from gambling. Sinful money made by cheating and dishonesty will not stay with you and will always lead to bad karma. Easy come, easy go, as they say ... you should only make money through honest means.

When I think about how I became the most successful of my siblings, I believe it is about the chemistry and mentality of each individual. My eldest brother was very intelligent, but he fell in with the wrong crowd. Indeed, all my siblings were intelligent—I was not any more or less intelligent than them—but I was lucky I had the structure and discipline of the Scouts during my formative years, where I spent most of my time exploring in nature and having fun learning skills in the outdoors rather than thinking about gambling and other destructive activities. If children make it to adulthood without falling into the wrong crowd, it is a big achievement. It is very easy to be influenced by negativity, particularly when you are an impressionable teenager.

Family Values

My mother, who was a very religious Buddhist and believed in karma, protected me and mostly set a good example. Having parents with good values gave me a strong foundation, and I brought my children up with the same values. Unlike me, they were born into privilege and financial security, but they grew up with my mother living with our family for over thirty-five years before she sadly passed away. They were also able to learn a lot from her, and I am very happy that kindness, generosity, and love for others come very naturally to all my children. If you are not brought up with a caring mindset, it is very difficult to teach these qualities, but I believe my children have it ingrained in them inherently.

They have always been able to differentiate between right and wrong, despite having had the freedom to travel the world and study in the UK, the United States, and China. They grew up in Ipoh, where I went to secondary school and where I met my wife, until they moved to England. Their time in Ipoh was long enough to consolidate a foundation of strong family values. They then went to respective colleges and universities in different countries around the world, but despite the many influences they came across, they have still held on to the values they learned in Ipoh. I ensured they were brought up to have a good work ethic and the desire to be successful and respected in their own right. They realized they have to work very hard in business to become personally successful and to earn people's respect.

Wherever I go, people show me respect and trust, and they have faith in me. Growing up, my children saw that these values—respect, trust, and faith—are also very important. They learned the importance of developing and attracting these three qualities, not only as a family but also as individuals.

Transformation Through Education

My classmates had already been focusing on education for their first six years of primary school, giving them a head start over me when I moved to lower secondary school. But having gained confidence in my geography results because I had an interest and passion for it, I thought, "Why not apply the same formula in all subjects?" True enough, this gave me the determination and stamina to work very hard to catch up with my peers, and I ended up achieving good grades in all subjects. At secondary school it became clear that I had to strengthen my educational foundation and my ability to absorb new knowledge to sharpen up the skills required for tertiary education and to make me more competitive in the job market or as a future entrepreneur.

No matter what career you wish to pursue, you need the foundation that education provides, especially if you don't come from a wealthy, educated family and don't have the financial support or past experience of other family members to help elevate you to the next level in academia. I come from a background of limited opportunities, so I had to focus on improving my education, and it was very tough. I didn't have anyone I aspired to be like when it came to my career; I just followed my heart and worked my way toward what I wanted to achieve.

Similarly, when I started playing among professional polo players, I was a complete beginner. I struggled to stay on the horse without falling off, let alone hitting the ball as well! Meanwhile I was competing with players who were so natural on a horse that they didn't even think about the riding element of polo. Scoring goals was second nature to them.

Somehow I managed to pass my lower secondary exams with good results at a small rural government English primary and secondary school in Bagan Serai. This enabled me to transfer to Saint Michael's Institution, the top school in the state capital, Ipoh, for the next stage of my education. Saint Michael's was an all-boys, government-aided secondary day school with mixed A-level classes, run by an Irish missionary. It was regarded as one of the best schools in the region in a wide range of academic and sports fields.

Life in Ipoh

Moving to Ipoh was a life-changing experience. In the 1960s it was one of the most vibrant cities in the country, driven by tin mining. The city also boasted the highest number of Mercedes cars in the country. It had the best nightlife, restaurants, and social scene at that time. This move opened my eyes to what living in a bustling city was like and caused me to change my perspective on many things, including wealth and finances.

Growing up in a very remote area, I had not needed much money to get by with, and up until that point, I had lived what I thought was a joyous life. But living in the city broadened my horizons, because if I had not moved to Ipoh, I would still be in my small hometown in Bagan Serai. None of what I've achieved in healthcare and business would have even crossed my mind, as my ambition and hunger for knowledge would not have been expanded, and I would never have known what else was out there for me.

When I began my lower secondary education and started to focus on more serious studying, two fundamental things changed in my life. First, after living in the countryside for fifteen years, I realized I needed a monthly allowance to live in a city, and I had to keep to a budget. Second, I saw people living much more extravagantly than I was, and it opened my eyes to how important it was for me to be successful in my education so I could improve my economic situation and future lifestyle.

My family had lived frugally and made just enough to survive, but in our small town of Bagan Serai, food and essentials didn't cost much, and there were not many expenses or outgoings for most families. Clothes, toys, and schoolbooks were passed down from one child to the next.

When you live in a city, you don't have as much of an outdoor life readily available. You have to travel to the countryside and pay to do recreational activities such as playing sports or exploring nature. In Ipoh it became clear that everything you do for recreation required money, and there were a lot of temptations to spend. In the city the cost of living was more than in the countryside, and I was also surrounded by more successful people with a more lavish lifestyle, such as my classmates all living in impressive houses and arriving at school in chauffeur-driven Mercedes, Alfa Romeos, Volvos, and other fancy cars. My eyes were opened to what money can buy, as in small country villages, you don't see this level of wealth. Some of my peers rode large CC motorcycles, while I only had a bicycle to get me from A to B.

While I started to aspire to elevate my own lifestyle, I was never jealous of people with money; I was inspired to be successful so I could also have my own assets, such as a nice car and a big house. I was also lucky that, even though my classmates were much more affluent than I was, most of them were friendly and seemed warm to me because, despite coming from a different background than them, I had a charismatic charm and was personable. Generally, they never looked down on me, perhaps because they saw me as a sincere, polite, small-town boy. They took care of me, respected me, and enjoyed having me around. When they invited me to their grand houses, it gave me a benchmark that motivated me to work hard to reach their level of affluence one day.

Being good with people and being a likable person are perhaps two of the most important qualities you can have when building a business, as everything comes down to dealing with people. It is quite easy to be likable in your school days when you have few responsibilities, but when you go into business, you can become paranoid about people's motives. If you are not paranoid, you're probably naive, and when you're naive, people will take advantage of you. It is a tricky balance.

Higher Education Journey

My graduation journey had certainly been very different from most of my peers. During my school era, tertiary education was a luxury; it was not for the masses. Telling others how many of your children had been to university was like telling them how wealthy you were or how intelligent your family was. Studying at a university in the Western world, particularly in the United Kingdom, was very prestigious, as we were a colony. Meanwhile gaining admission to a local university showed you must have a record of excellent academic results, especially if you were non-Malay.

Helping out my parents in our family business was more important than my education. In those days we didn't have foreign workers, and we had very limited employees—irrespective of what work needed to be done—so everyone in my family had to be hands on. Nowadays we would describe children selling fruit at the roadside as exploiting child labor! However, it proved to be a useful apprenticeship for me.

When it came to deciding on a career plan, caring for others was always my motivation. Even though I aimed to make money, I always wanted to become a doctor because I felt it suited my personality, as I love taking care of people. My mother was very generous and loving, and she liked to look after people, so it seems I inherited these genes from her, and it is almost like it was in my DNA to go into a caring profession.

After I studied at Saint Michael's, my results qualified me to go to university. I therefore went on to study for a doctor of medicine at the University of Santo Tomas, another mission institution renowned for its medical school. Santo Tomas is twenty-five years older than

Harvard, founded by the same missionaries who established Harvard University in America, so it was run under an American system.

I completed a premedical course, then I finished a bachelor's degree, before I started an MD (doctor of medicine). Initially, while I was studying overseas, my mom gave me RM200 per month to help me with my expenses. This was the equivalent of $50 and below the poverty line. But when I finished my first year of the MD program, my family couldn't afford for me to continue. My brother-in-law wrote me a letter to let me know that my parents could not afford to continue funding my education. While it was extremely disappointing, it didn't come as a big surprise to me. I had no choice but to leave and look for a scholarship if I wanted to finish my higher education.

In hindsight it worked out for the best, as I went on to get an ASEAN Science and Technology Fellowship to study a postgraduate degree in medical microbiology in Kuala Lumpur, where I was even paid to study! Plus I was given accommodation and provided with three meals a day. I couldn't believe my luck.

I also got accepted by Singapore University and the London School of Hygiene & Tropical Medicine for a master's in public health, but I couldn't afford to go to either of these. The ASEAN Science and Technology Fellowship program included a collective of countries in Southeast Asia offering different tropical disease courses, and from being in the second batch of postgraduates in 1979 right up until today, I have remained the youngest graduate with a postgraduate diploma in medical microbiology, having been just twenty-one years old at the time.

One day my mom was upset with me, and she told me if she hadn't helped finance my education, she would have been very rich and could have bought a lucrative rubber estate. It was a lot of money for her then, but I joked the return on investment on me would be more than a thousandfold. When I went back home for Chinese New Year one year with the monthly fellowship allowance for my scholarship, I gave all the money to my mom. It meant I had to go one month without any pocket money, but I cried with happiness as I gave her money for the first time in my life. I was so pleased I could give something back to her. It was a very special feeling that will never leave me. I didn't see it as a sacrifice; it felt satisfying that I could make my mom happy and give her the chance to celebrate her Chinese New Year with a bit of extra cash.

Nowadays this is nothing to me, but it is all relative. At the time I gave away everything I had, and it was a feeling that will always stay with me. Thankfully, I didn't starve, as I could still go to the canteen for all my meals. But I know that no matter how poor she was, my mother would have pawned every piece of her limited jewelry collection to help others if they needed emergency money. She really had a heart of gold. As the youngest child, I spent the most time with her, and after I had finished studying, she lived with me for over thirty-five years. So we spent fifty years of our lives together.

As it was the holiday season, getting the train back from Bagan Serai to Kuala Lumpur was extremely cramped and busy, with all the passengers packed into the carriages like sardines for the whole journey. There were no seats whatsoever, so I had to stand for hours, but even this uncomfortable journey could not diminish the pleasure I felt about having been able to give back to my mom.

Dr. Beh Chun Chuan with Steve Forbes

Chapter 2

BECOMING A BUSINESS OWNER

I didn't hesitate to work for myself and run my own business rather than work for someone else. I grew up in a business-minded family, so doing business is in my DNA. Once I was on the pathway to making money for myself, I realized I thrive on challenges and embrace stress—I am always on the go and can never sit around doing nothing. Despite my living a more hectic life than the rest of my family, they are all very proud of me.

Growing up, my family was looked down upon, and it became my aim to earn respect for them. Today my hometown, state, and country are all proud of what I have achieved, and I aim to continue making them proud.

Entering the Workforce: Microbiology and Early Challenges

In 1979 I began my first job as a certified microbiologist in a private food testing laboratory. I guaranteed my boss I could secure the necessary laboratory accreditation and license. At the time certified medical microbiologists were rare, and every food material destined for export needed to be tested.

I earned full accreditation as a medical microbiologist from the Institute for Medical Research in Kuala Lumpur through the ASEAN Science and Technology Fellowship. By 1980 my boss entrusted me with managing both the private hospital pathology lab and the food testing lab. Therefore, within one year, I was working two jobs, overseeing the two companies, and being paid two salaries. However, I was more interested in the medical labs, where honesty and transparency are essential and can never be compromised, rather than food testing. I always believed in making an honest living and sincerely helping people.

There is a big difference between the mindsets in medical labs and food labs. You have to be honest in the medical sector. In medical testing you must always be transparent and truthful, as the results of a test can never be compromised. In contrast the food testing industry is more about making a profit. Given a choice I have always preferred to do what I am passionate about and what I care about; therefore working in the medical sector was more suited to my character, nature, and interests.

In the late 1970s and early 1980s, many people still did not know what medical laboratory testing was. In Chinese culture, they used to say gambling is in your blood, but until today I still do not have a blood test to detect gamblers, so it must be a myth.

While I decided to focus on medical pathology labs and based myself in a hospital, I still continued overseeing the food testing lab. As a certified microbiologist, my signature and supervision were needed to certify that food products were fit for human consumption.

Building Experience and Relationships

After just fourteen months of working in the job, I had made the food testing company very profitable by taking on multiple roles—lab analysis, sales and marketing, accounts, PR, logistics and the collection of samples and money. Even though the location of my laboratory was far away from the major food factories, they still chose to work with me, as we had a similar Teochew clanship that connected us.

My boss saw I was very capable and dedicated, so he suggested I buy out the company. As well as having the laboratories, my boss was a certified chemist who provided contract manufacturing of multipurpose household cleaning products. When he got a huge original equipment manufacturer contract to produce Shelltox, he wanted to concentrate on his manufacturing business, and he asked me to take over the labs.

This period was also pivotal in my personal life. My boss often invited me to his house, where he was manufacturing cleaning products in his backyard, and he asked me to go over to help in the evenings. I didn't usually have evening plans in those days, so I had nothing to lose by helping him out and learning some new skills in a different industry. I used to go to his house after having an early dinner, and he would play mah-jongg with a group of his friends, including my now brother-in-law, who wanted to introduce me to his younger sister, Datin Poh Lay See. He saw me as a pleasant, hardworking young man and arranged a dinner for the two of us to meet. One year later we got married and moved into her family house with her parents, and the rest is history, as they say. We have now been happily married for over forty-five years with four amazing children.

I was very grateful to my boss for entrusting me with his two laboratory businesses, as I learned a lot about managing laboratories, operating them, and investing. I also met my wife because of him.

Strategic Business Decisions

Even though there was a lot of money in the food testing lab, I chose not to buy that company. I only bought the medical testing lab, which in the long run helped me gain a better, more genuine reputation. In the food testing lab, there was a lot of pressure from food factories. As soon as the samples arrived, the factories wanted results as soon as possible so they could cash out the letter of credit and the goods could load for shipment to meet overseas customer deadlines. Factories are not interested in conducting microbiology testing, but overseas buyers require the tests to fulfill their respective countries' stipulated quality standards, ensuring the products are safe and fit for consumption.

I didn't feel comfortable with the working culture in the food testing sector, so when I only bought the medical testing lab, my boss asked me to guarantee I would never set up a competitive food testing lab in the same town, and I gave him my word. After more than twenty years, we set up BP Healthcare Group Food Testing Lab in Butterworth, Penang, long after my boss's original food testing lab in Ipoh had closed down.

From Science to Leadership

In 1981 I made the leap to business ownership, coining myself a "scientist-preneur." I had already gotten a master of business administration from Golden Gate University, San Francisco, in the early 1980s while I was starting out with my own business, which helped me understand accounting and enabled me to formulate the strategy for my business plan.

My postgraduate microbiology dean was a very genuine person, and he was like a mentor to me. While he was still in government service, he informed me the Ministry of Health would be introducing the Private Pathology Lab Act to regulate and license medical pathology labs. The law was starting to catch up in healthcare, and the government would soon pass laws and acts that I would be required to factor into my business as it grew. I took these tips from my dean on board, and while also serving my customers, I started all the accreditation and certification processes to prepare for new laws to pass.

I found out that meeting government regulatory approval often took a lot of time, and for a young entrepreneur who was eager to set up a new operation, it was a slow process to get it fully up and running. Because of my preparedness, once I had taken on the company, I was able to expand my business without coming up against any major issues with the law. We already had systems and procedures approved and in place ahead of our competitors, which was a huge benefit.

Establishing BP Healthcare Group

I had already secured the funds to complete the buyout in 1980, but to make it auspicious, I signed the agreement on January 1, 1981, so I always remember how many years I've been my own boss. The name BP Healthcare Group stands for my surname, "Beh," and my wife's maiden name, "Poh." When I first named the business, we were not yet married, but I had already combined our names so she would be a partner in the company.

I officially did the management buyout on January 1, 1981. To complete the buyout, I had to borrow 100 percent of the funds from the bank. In those days you had to pitch to the bank for a loan like a start-up, and it was purely based on character financing, as I had no collateral to pledge to the bank. The bankers evaluated my skills and work ethic, and even though I hadn't prepared a presentation or speech, they could tell I was very knowledgeable in my field and passionate about my business.

I was a trained and educated scientist, but I didn't have any experience with finance at that time. So when they asked if I wanted an overdraft or term loan, I didn't know what the difference was. I just needed the money! Because the bankers felt I was hardworking, committed, and trustworthy, they suggested that a fixed repayment scheme over a five-year repayment plan would be the best option. The bank swiftly approved 100 percent of the loan, and I got the money I needed. Within two and a half years, I had paid it off completely.

Growth and Vision

What started as one medical pathology lab in Ipoh, named BP Healthcare Group Clinical Laboratories in 1980, grew over the years to become the BP Healthcare Group, and I expanded the company nationwide.

We now operate more than 120 outlets, offering the following services: medical pathology laboratories integrating a cluster of diverse primary care facilities across Malaysia, secondary care and tertiary care, over fifty pharmacies and dispensaries, fifty diagnostic centers, special dental clinics, hearing aid centers, specialist day care centers, an eye specialist clinic, fifty food and environmental testing centers, medical waste incineration plants, in-house research and development of medical software, and the sale of various medical software systems. We are a one-stop cohesive healthcare solution with interlinked support from all the companies within the BP Healthcare Group.

I sometimes describe our services like going to the supermarket. A 7-Eleven convenience store doesn't give you a full, complete range of products, but it can satisfy your immediate needs. Around ten years ago, BP Healthcare Group had become the indisputable leader in primary and secondary care, but we have since achieved my dream of upgrading to be a Walmart of the healthcare industry, offering a full range of services, including tertiary care, to be considered a hypermarket in the sector. We have served more than eight figures of customers to date and are still counting.

To look at it in the simplest way, when you compare my service apples to apples, I am always trying to be better than everyone else, not only by offering apples but also oranges and grapes, and cross-selling the services at the most competitive price in the same outlet. I have all the infrastructure, the facilities, and the digital platform to make things cost-effective and straightforward.

How did I achieve such exponential growth? The key has been to remain agile and ready to capitalize on opportunities by moving with the times, listening to what customers want, and investing in the most cutting-edge technology to keep improving and expanding our services. This has enabled us to offer revolutionary healthcare solutions before our competitors. Starting in the early 1980s, it was the simple human approach of giving my time and resources to offer free health screenings to people in need that gained me a reputation for being compassionate and laid the foundations of building a business that cares.

Laureus Polo Cup, United Kingdom

Chapter 3

REVOLUTIONIZING THE HEALTHCARE MODEL

One of the first things I did to promote my health screening and testing services in the early days was going to patients rather than having them come to me. Every weekend I traveled around the country in a mobile unit doing health screening campaigns for free. I pretty much worked with every big organization in Malaysia, including the Lions Club, Rotary Club, churches, temples, NGOs, and political parties. Along the way I gained a good reputation, and BP Healthcare Group became known as a company that cares for people and provides quality services and timely results.

Back in those days, though, people were often very apprehensive when you offered them something for free, especially in healthcare. To start with, they didn't want it. Many Malaysians were reluctant to go for health screenings even if it was free, because they feared knowing about underlying diseases. They preferred that ignorance was bliss!

Doing social work, in hindsight, was the best marketing and promotion I could have done. BP Healthcare Group became a household name, gaining word-of-mouth recommendations. I was known for being reliable, and I always delivered the highest standards at a reasonable price, so anyone who needed healthcare services started coming to BP Healthcare Group. This reputation for reliability and quality service, built through countless hours of community work, would prove essential as Malaysian attitudes toward healthcare began to evolve.

Shifting Attitudes Toward Health

Over time attitudes began to shift. Today most Malaysians with secure incomes are concerned about their health. If they suspect there is any underlying abnormality or illness, they like to have early or preventative treatment as soon as possible. This shows how people's priorities change when they are financially secure and live a comfortable lifestyle, allowing them to afford to care more about their health. Many of those people who reluctantly attended my free screenings in the past now willingly pay for more comprehensive health screening packages.

Doing social work, in hindsight, was the best marketing and promotion I could have done. BP Healthcare Group became a household name, gaining word-of-mouth recommendations. I was known for being reliable, and I always delivered the highest standards at a reasonable price, so anyone who needed healthcare services started coming to BP Healthcare Group. This reputation for reliability and quality service, built through countless hours of community work, would prove essential as Malaysian attitudes toward healthcare began to evolve.

Rather than targeting vast urban areas such as Kuala Lumpur, I tried to reach all areas of society, not only operating in cities but often going deep into the countryside too. I offered tests and treatments, including deworming, to people working on farms in rural areas, who were at risk of picking up parasitic infections and becoming anemic. Often, farmers suffered from extreme tiredness, not knowing they had a parasitic infection, which could easily be treated with deworming. Following treatment they made a full recovery and stopped suffering from fatigue due to anemia.

I did a lot of charity work in the early days, and I worked seven days a week without ever mentioning money. Over time word about BP Healthcare Group spread, and my business grew so much that we had to go nationwide to meet the needs of all the rural communities we were serving. When I was running just one operation, I was doing very well, and the cash flow was good, as money was coming in, and I didn't have many outgoings. I was making enough positive cash flow to purchase more assets and reinvest in equipment and digital technology.

But after a while, the roots and trunk of the business in Ipoh had grown in such a way that I realized I needed to branch out to be able to absorb more sun and more water to keep it thriving. I had support from people around me, such as my brothers, to open more outlets in different locations. I developed a chain of outlets, and before long there was one of my health testing labs in every major town and city in Malaysia, and customers started requesting additional services.

Expanding the Healthcare Network

Following the first successful outlet in Ipoh, a hospital-based lab, the second outlet opened in Taiping. It was also based in a hospital, owned by my friend, an obstetrician and gynecologist. This location was less than one hour north of Ipoh and a similar distance south of my hometown of Bagan Serai.

My third outlet was an independent laboratory in Penang. I had always wanted to live in Penang, as it was a childhood dream of mine to stay on the island there with beautiful beaches, as I love being by the sea. My first-ever job offer was in Penang, and I was keen to go there, but at the last minute, I was informed there was no longer a job vacancy, so I accepted my second job offer in Ipoh instead.

When I started to expand the chain of outlets even further across the country, it actually became more difficult to fail than it was to succeed. The more outlets we opened, the more income and manpower we had, and I had many multitasking members of staff, so I never had acute staff shortages. More outlets meant I could move staff between outlets to cover staff shortages in any of the locations. Today all businesses in all sectors have one main issue: not having enough manpower. But at BP Healthcare Group our staff have been trained to have multiple skill sets so they can be adaptable and apply their various skills wherever they are needed most and to cover colleagues on leave.

When you scale up and have a chain of outlets, the most important thing is to standardize all operations and equipment to make sure all outlets are under the same standard operating procedures. Operating services with consistency enables staff to move between outlets and be familiar with all the equipment and not have to learn how to use new equipment they have never used before. Staff being unfamiliar with equipment can lead to examinations taking longer to complete and can increase the likelihood of machine breakdowns, errors in examinations, and legal suits, which will result in burning the company's pocket and giving you sleepless nights. What's more, whichever services you offer must be executed in exactly the same way so the patient has the same high standard of experience in any location they might visit. The results must always be presented in the same user-friendly format so they are simple to interpret and compare with previous results.

Today we have now opened so many outlets in Malaysia, opening a new clinic is like a walk in the park for us. Each time we open a new outlet, I have a team of people who know exactly what services are required and in which locations we should open. We also have dedicated teams for logistics, licensing, engineering, and manpower. Money-wise we have no problems, as we use our internal funds, but in the early days, it was more challenging when we wanted to set up more services.

Back then, if we needed to spend a lot of money on setting up new services, we used bank loans or hire purchases to secure all the necessary equipment or fixtures we needed. Sometimes we needed to buy the property, knowing that we could generate enough revenue from it to pay back the loan. The most important thing for most people is having the capital to set up a new venture, but this was never an issue for me. I never had any issues securing a loan or cash flow for repayment, as I had a trustworthy reputation and a constant income. While waiting for approval on new outlets, I always directed my newly recruited employees to existing operating outlets to brush up their skills. That way, as soon as the new outlet was ready, they could hit the ground running, and no time would be wasted. While the physical expansion was crucial, I recognized that the future of healthcare wouldn't just be about location; it would also be about innovation and staying ahead of technological advances.

Staying Ahead: Following the Line of Innovation

Just as in polo, where players must anticipate and stay on the optimal line of the ball to maintain control and momentum, in healthcare, success comes from anticipating and adapting to technological advances. When I founded BP Healthcare Group in the late 1970s, it was an exciting time for developments in healthcare. There were many multinational medical equipment suppliers coming up with new technology, and I jumped onto the bandwagon and rode with them. Like a polo player who reads the game and positions themselves ahead of the play, I positioned BP Healthcare Group to embrace emerging technologies before our competitors.

When I first began working in the healthcare industry in the late 1970s, healthcare was run using very manual systems. This meant many processes were time-consuming and inefficient, and there were a lot of preanalytical, analytical, and transcription errors. We were still working and doing everything offline. It was only after I had been working for ten to fifteen years that we even had basic fax machines, let alone the internet! This was fine when the volume of business was small and testing was routine. It was not difficult; it was just tedious.

There was a test we used to do to check thyroid function. In those days it was done using a radioactive method with radioactive assays with no gloves, without knowing the extent of the danger of radiation. I would start this testing process at 8:00 or 9:00 a.m., and by the time I finished doing the tests, I would be waiting for my then-girlfriend (now wife) to pick me up to go for lunch. Back then thyroid tests were so time-consuming I could only do limited tests per day, but as the volume of patients picked up, it became vital to speed up.

When I founded BP Healthcare Group, it was just a small laboratory, and I was very fortunate that in the late 1970s, it was an exciting time for developments in healthcare. There were a lot of multinational medical equipment suppliers coming up with new technology, and I jumped onto the bandwagon and rode with them. There was a global trend where healthcare systems started to use more technology, going from manual systems to semiautomation, then eventually fully automated. With technology, I followed what began as a tiny seed, until it grew into a very large tree. And it is still growing. Today full automation makes processes scalable, and millions of tests can be done per day with a digitally linked patient walk-away system, ensuring there is no chance of transcription errors.

The Digital Transformation

A big part of my success is that I am evolving my business along with advances in technology, which has not only increased efficiency, productivity, and accuracy for my company, but it has also enabled me to still be in full control of operations with a five-figure workforce from anywhere in the world. I just require a connection to the internet. This means that despite having so much to oversee, I still have time to travel the world and pursue my passion for playing polo internationally, because I am able to seamlessly run BP Healthcare Group 24/7, 365 days per year by managing everything online from wherever I am. Even on a trip to Antarctica with SpaceX …

Today there are so many distractions when running a business, but as a good leader, I always prioritize communicating well with my team and my employees. I always say, even if I had to teach a group of idiots, I could still ensure they get straight As. One of my key skills is being able to simplify things and communicate so my instructions are easy for people to understand. Clear communication skills is one of the main reasons why my company runs so successfully, and I am always looking for new ways to improve and update my communication systems across my company.

There was nothing particularly outstanding about me and my aptitude for technology; I was merely a willing and open-minded participant in modernizing the healthcare industry. I was confident that technology could benefit my company, so I embraced it and got a head start with the aim of providing a better service for customers. Each year I still give provision for technology advancement capital expenditures to ensure BP Healthcare Group is always leading from the front in technology. I had to invest a lot in the early days to keep up with rapid development, but while I was investing and embracing new technology, many competitors were too scared to invest in it at all, resulting in them falling behind.

To give a polo analogy, utilizing new technology was like being given the best and fastest horses to play a match on. These horses will always be able to outrun and outmaneuver the horses on the opposing team, so you will have a much better chance of scoring, making it almost impossible for you not to win.

Diversifying Healthcare Services

In the 1970s and early 1980s, patients would usually go to a clinic or a hospital for health tests and get referred to specialists; they didn't go directly to a laboratory for tests. However, I overturned the standard procedure and enabled patients to come directly to me at my testing laboratories. I started recruiting doctors, so all my testing centers were also clinics called diagnostic centers, which I owned and ran alongside the testing laboratory.

I could have stuck with running the medical lab and grown it nationwide, and I would have made more than enough money to live happily and comfortably with my wife and children. However, there are a lot of traps you can fall into if you are just running one singular business in healthcare. As my first boss had warned me, there were a lot of government regulatory bodies coming in that restricted what medical labs would be able to do.

The Birth of BP Healthcare Group Diagnostic Centre

What's more, at the turn of the twentieth century, people started to learn about wellness and take an interest in it. I knew that doing blood tests alone would not be enough. I set up a diagnostic center in 2000, when I amalgamated all my companies into one group and called it BP Healthcare Group Diagnostic Centre. This was a first in Malaysia. We contributed to health tourism in the area of travel health and vaccinations, and we also offered head-to-toe medical examinations. Our business for checking the wellness of healthy people was actually much more sizable than the market for treating sick people. There is a reason why prevention is better than cure …

Labs needed the support of an in-house doctor to meet all the regulatory requirements. However, when we extended to running the diagnostic center and a medical laboratory, we realized the doctors themselves were not very accomplished when it came to dispensing medicines, and the standard wasn't good enough for us. That is why we introduced our own pharmacies for all our outlets, so medication had to pass through trained pharmacists, creating another firewall before the patient received the medication.

Expanding into Pharmacy Services

In 1995 I started BP Healthcare Group Pharmacy, a small, independent pharmacy that thrived in the wholesale business. Fast-forward to 2011, my daughter Lovy, a pharmacist with a degree from the UCL School of Pharmacy and experience working in Singapore, returned to Malaysia. Inspired by her global perspective, I established Lovy Pharmacy in her name in 2011.

This was not just a pharmacy; it was Lovy's chance to build a legacy and create a chain that would revolutionize pharmacy practice in Malaysia. With her international experience and commitment to excellence, Lovy knew she had to set the bar high—after all, her name and reputation were at stake.

Since it was founded, Lovy Pharmacy has been at the forefront of innovation in Malaysia, being among the first to offer online ordering and delivery, consultations via video calls, eco-friendly practices in its pharmacies, and the first drive-through pharmacy in the country. Lovy Pharmacy also provides other enhanced services, including compounding pharmacies, cataract finders, sexual health services, and mental health consultations.

Identifying and Filling Market Gaps

One after another, we realized many other healthcare companies were not offering services of a high enough standard, because of a lack of necessary experience in their workforces. For example, there were not many healthcare centers offering specialist advice and care for hearing problems, so when we started a dedicated hearing center, it became the biggest hearing center in Malaysia, and we filled it with patients almost overnight. There was also a lack of clinics for drivers to do sleep tests in preparation for commercial driving license assessments for JPJ, the road transport department for Malaysia, so we launched sleep clinics to prevent driving accidents caused by drivers falling asleep at the wheel.

We responded not only to government requirements but also to market requirements and trends. We held a panel for a lot of multinational companies, and it became clear they had a lot of health requirements for their employees. However, many hospitals did not cater to them, as hospital operating costs are so high. Perhaps for some clinics and hospitals, the return would be too small to invest a lot in giving staff special training, but for BP Healthcare Group, offering niche services if customers required them was worth it, as we had the resources. Our operating costs are approximately 10 percent of any hospital, so we are able to offer certain low-cost examinations and still make a small margin. In healthcare every registered patient incurs a minimum cost, but some hospitals don't offer such low-cost services on which they won't make much of a margin. Our main focus is providing quality services that are as affordable as possible for the patient.

Because of this, we established a very large customer base. Whether it's a sick patient, a healthy individual wanting to know their health status, companies needing to check prospective employees' health before employing them, or companies checking the health of staff already working under stress to show they care about the welfare of their employees, all can engage BP Healthcare Group to help.

This gave me an advantage, as other competitive healthcare providers at the time were running singular primary care services, such as laboratories, clinics, or pharmacies, but no one else was offering all these services from one outlet provider.

After offering pathology, medical services, specialist services including sleep clinics and hearing clinics, doctors, and a pharmacy, we then added radiology equipment, including CT scans. Some of my centers also offered secondary care with operating theaters, not just primary care. BP Healthcare Group was now able to provide all the services of a hospital nationwide around Malaysia; the only difference was we didn't have inpatients.

As the company grew, we were able to offer more services to patients, and I had essentially selected the best and most profitable operational departments of a hospital. I was offering customers multiple services within one outlet, becoming "omnipresent" in the country. I also set up courier services, so I was in full control of sample collections, transportation, and delivery and could ensure a quicker turnaround time for results. It is very important to preserve sample integrity, as the result you produce is only as good as your sample integrity.

Customer-Driven Growth

Developing and continually upgrading our internal software has also been a critical part of progressing BP Healthcare Group over the years. When my youngest son, Garvy, was still studying in the United States in 2011, he told me that the server-based system we were using was too slow and could easily be hacked, and he asked if we could change it to being cloud based. At first I was skeptical, but he explained to me that if all our information was spread across different parts of the world, it is more difficult for hackers to get complete information. I agreed to try it, and we started with Microsoft, Google, and Apple, and now all our software is run on the cloud. Our first in-house laboratory information system software was very simple, and we also started using mobile phones instead of computer-based systems or pen and paper. So when COVID-19 hit in 2019, we were already using online applications, which gave us a head start.

Once we had designed our own software for our group, we then sold it to other clinics to use. Now thousands of clinics around the country are using my software, making it a good passive income. At the beginning I was giving out free software and hardware and paying monthly connectivity fees to gain customer loyalty. In those days, besides the CPU, one monitor alone cost RM10,000.

We were one of the first healthcare providers to introduce an online system and e-commerce, where patients could simply log in to our website to book an appointment. This was particularly useful for clinics and hospitals, as they could see the progress of tests in real time to track the status of which tests were completed and which were pending. Once your company is digitized, your customer will have a more seamless experience with reduced waiting times. But it isn't enough to just have the technology there; the systems also have to be user-friendly for both patients and healthcare providers.

Our patients are able to look at their results and either book an appointment to see a doctor in the clinic, have a tele/video consultation, consult their family physician, or use healthcare AI for further advice. In addition, if medication is needed, Lovy Pharmacy is also able to give patients teleconsultations, prescriptions, and medicine delivery.

It was also my policy that customers and prospective customers had a program where they could view my pharmacy products and prices and compare them with competitors. BP Healthcare Group prices were the benchmark—if they could find the same product a lot cheaper, then they could buy it elsewhere, but if we were the cheapest, which we often were, they would buy from us. We don't restrict customers from buying from any other companies if our price is not competitive, as we have an open system, and this has built trust at BP Healthcare Group.

However, in the beginning, when I offered a free clinic software system, many clinics dared not use it. Even though it was server based in their clinic only, they still thought I could steal their data. Some people thought we had a hidden agenda, but in time more people who used our software were happy with the service. This meant more people had confidence in us, so we were able to sell more systems around the country, and it went from being a start-up cost center to a profit-generating center.

We constantly upgraded and improved our software using CPUs and notebooks, and in 2014 Garvy developed the "Doctor2U" app in the same year he graduated, enabling customers to connect with BP Healthcare Group services on their mobile phone. We looked at business trends at the time and saw young people in particular did not just want a brick-and-mortar service where they had to travel to see doctors in our clinics. We gave them the option of being able to go online to Doctor2U to request tests, results, consultations, and access advice at their fingertips 24/7.

This new technology improved the system we already had. Garvy made it into an app form, progressing it from a computer platform to an iPhone platform. Now our customers can see their medical records and test results, book services and make payments, and schedule sample collections from the palm of their hand, which saves a lot of time. We have a fleet of in-house lorries, vans, and motorbikes that can collect samples from people's homes. Either you can book a collection when one of our couriers is in your area, or if it is urgent, you can book a special collection. You can also track the status of the sample so you know when it is collected, on the way to the lab, pending results in the lab, and when the results are in. We create barcodes so the samples never get mixed up.

To keep up with new changes and movements that are affecting the healthcare industry, I have been attending the Forbes Healthcare Summit in New York with my family since the inaugural event in 2012, along with other captains of the healthcare industry. I remember the idea of "Uber Care" coming up and being discussed years ago, and this is essentially about on-demand care, which we had the foresight to offer through Doctor2U. Like an Uber Taxi, it is quick and efficient to book via your smartphone.

Doctor2U has not only brought access to quicker healthcare but has also helped educate people in Malaysia about healthcare, as millions of patients register every year and receive access to trusted, professional medical advice from wherever they are. They are also directed to the best BP Healthcare Group outlet to go to for their specific needs.

We always thank our customers for some of our growth, as they often give us feedback and make suggestions about how we can do better to serve them, and we listen. After Garvy had started the Doctor2U app, clients started asking how they could order medication, so we added that service to the app as well. Every time customers complain about something, we take it as a positive rather than fighting back, as their input helps us make improvements. We believe that the customer is king and that they are always right. If we went to an international consulting agency to ask them how we could improve, it would be extremely expensive.

When I offer a service, I think patients have the right to complain. I like getting feedback from them, because if there is something they are not happy about and they don't say anything and walk out of the door, I have just lost a customer forever. What's more, as per the sales rule of 250, coined by Joe Girard, if you make a mistake and a patient is unhappy, they might tell 250 people negative news. However, if the patient is happy, they might encourage 250 people to use your services. We view patient complaints as a chance to improve. Every piece of feedback is an opportunity for us to reflect, learn, and make necessary adjustments to ensure that we are meeting the needs of our patients.

Beyond Healthcare: Environmental and Food Testing

Another area we now work in is food and environmental testing, as we realized some of the companies and factories we were already providing healthcare services to also needed food testing and other testing services. Many BP Healthcare Group outlets and supporting clinics using our healthcare services had links to the food industry and recommended us.

Likewise, some owners of corporate companies such as factories and importers, whom BP Healthcare Group was already working with in the food industry, realized we also offer medical services and food testing. We had many corporate clients who would request our services for medical examinations for staff doing food handling and factory processing, who also needed us to test their food products. So we did food testing for the factory and health tests for food handlers. BP Healthcare Group can work with any type of business and offer a holistic service. We started food testing nationwide and went on to offer environmental testing for water, waste, noise, and air.

Today we do all sorts of testing. Everything we eat must be tested, everything that is imported or exported must be tested, and all raw materials and all the water we drink must be tested. The air where we live and work must be tested. Essentially everything in our everyday lives—how people eat and breathe and even the waste they produce—

relates back to our businesses. We help monitor and keep the world clean and safe for human habitation.

From the day you are born until the day you die, everyone can become my customer. The only thing we do not currently offer is a memorial service business for those who pass away. I stopped at that, but maybe it is something future generations will explore.

In Malaysia people have health insurance, and I also handle some insurance cases, even though those cases are not generally very lucrative, and payments are often delayed six to nine months. But offering health insurance means I don't need to give any commission to external insurers, doctors, or hospitals. When I work directly with customers without a middleman, I can then give the best price to benefit the patient.

Making Healthcare Affordable

These days healthcare is very expensive globally, so while some of our competitors are taking the opportunity to inflate prices, we are doing our best to try to squeeze prices and keep them low so our customers can still afford to live a good quality of life. Patients can lock in the best prices by buying healthcare packages for set periods, such as one-, five-, or ten-year contracts to avoid price increases caused by future inflation. They can also buy multiple packages to get further discounts for family members or company employees. For patients aged forty-five years old and above, we offer a lifetime head-to-toe package for RM35,000, which includes an annual full health screening for life.

Our pricing is designed in such a way that our packages are very competitive. For many healthcare competitors, especially hospitals, their main expense is finance charges, so they have high capital and operating expenses, while BP Healthcare Group has lower capital and operating costs. We make our profit by selling more services to our customers, earning less per customer but generating more volume. We can handle thousands of patients per day, yet we meet good turn-around times and ensure high-quality services at a fair price.

Because we started off as a laboratory, it has brought costs down a lot. We are not like other players in the market, where their entry prices are very high to begin with, because they have to pay back what they've spent. We are financially stable, so when thinking about the future of the company, we feel the sky is the limit.

Digital technology and AI have drastically reduced operating costs in terms of staff and consumption, so I believe the price of healthcare across the board should be coming down as a result of digitalization; it should not be going up. With the technological advancements we have now invented to accelerate processes and replace manual labor, today healthcare should be getting less expensive for patients.

For example, thanks to new technology, I can now sell the thyroid test that I mentioned previously for RM1 instead of RM7, and the user can seamlessly do the test, walk away, and receive the results shortly afterward, directly to their phone. With full automation we can now do millions of these tests annually with zero analysis and transcription errors. In contrast, with the old manual method, I was only able to do very few tests each year, and there was a high percentage of mistakes. This is why I question how healthcare can be getting more expensive.

Ultimately it is because third-party insurance companies and owners of hospitals are charging extortionate prices; reaping all the profit from the poor doctors, paramedics, and hospitals; and leaving crumbs. Private hospitals also want to make as much money as possible, which makes it unaffordable for most people.

I believe that the government should institutionalize healthcare and that it should not be owned by private individuals or corporations. In the past, in Japan, for example, hospitals were not allowed to be publicly listed, as once a company is listed, it operates for profit. At the same time, in Malaysia, the former finance minister, Tun Daim Zainuddin, rejected Pantai Hospital being listed, as he had similar beliefs as Japan—that hospitals should be institutions that care for the people, not ones focused on making money. Unfortunately without capitalism, the owners of private hospitals cannot improve and expand their services.

BP Healthcare Group is now a large group, so whenever we buy equipment, we buy fifty or one hundred units. Even big hospitals don't place an order of that quantity, and because of the economies of scale, I am able to negotiate a better price. We are the only company that can buy that many units, as our concept of standardization means we require exactly the same equipment or system in each of our outlets.

The privilege of buying in bulk is volume discount. Big brands sell to me, and then they can name-drop my company and say BP Healthcare Group is using their equipment all over the country. I am renowned for not being easy to please, as I have such high standards! People think if someone can sell to me, their equipment must be good quality. Whenever brands have a deal with me, they can then go all around the country using me as a testimony and making their sales pitches easier.

Maintaining Quality Standards

It has always been my approach that everything at BP Healthcare Group must be done to the highest standard possible. On the quality matter, we are not just talking about the human resources side but also our infrastructure and our equipment. For the people who work for me, we offer continuous medical education, sending our staff for regular training courses and to conferences to enable them to keep increasing their knowledge, continuous medical education, and continuous professional development. BP Healthcare Group was the first Asian company to secure laboratory accreditation from the Joint Commission International in the fifth cycle. We are also accredited by the International Organization for Standardization, showing we meet the highest international benchmarks of quality and operating standards.

People don't come to BP Healthcare Group to see a specific doctor; they come to us knowing they will be satisfied with any of our doctors, as all of them are trained to the same high standard. When patients walk into BP Healthcare Group, they know what is expected from the BP Healthcare Group brand in terms of price, quality, service, and turnaround time.

When you are renowned for the quality of your products and services, you are trusted, and people walk into your company comfortably and know what standards to expect. It is like walking into any Starbucks and getting a coffee—you know what you are going to get. We have set a standard, and that is why BP Healthcare Group has progressed from being a group of companies to being known as a brand.

The Future of Healthcare: AI and Beyond

While BP Healthcare Group is currently experiencing a period of continued growth, we also know there is an expiry date for every business, once it has run its life cycle. I believe that with new computer systems and the rise of AI, in the not-so-distant future, it will be possible for you to be informed of your health status every day at home in real time, and you will no longer need to go into a clinic or hospital for tests. These days patients have a lot more access to information, and it is not the patient who is scared to go to the doctor, but the other way around. Patients now have so much access to information that they usually go see the doctor armed with a self-diagnosis.

Wearable technology has also advanced hugely in the past few years, enabling people to monitor their own health information, such as glucose levels, at home. As a businessman, you must always keep looking for ways to improve. One day you are talking about what you are doing or going to do, then the next day technology or government regulation changes, and whatever you were doing the day before is now obsolete. You must always stay tuned to what is happening next. Don't be complacent with what you are doing now or be someone who thinks it "won't happen." It is already happening. And this could not be more true in the case of AI.

We think of AI happening far in the future, but this shift in the healthcare sector will happen sooner than people think. Technology develops so fast these days, and I believe healthcare costs will also start to come down even more with AI.

I remember talking to a telecom CEO over ten years ago, and he told me his business of SMS and fixed lines was dropping, because people had started using WhatsApp, which was free. So he had to look at how to reinvent the business to reconnect with lost customers and sales. This global trend changed the healthcare industry too.

Change is crucial for survival. It's not that I particularly want to change, but you have to adapt to survive. You can't keep running things in the same way without adapting to changes that are happening around you. You must keep your company forward thinking and relevant.

Take testing your heart as an example; thirty years ago it was done with blood tests and some electronic tests, and there were only four parameters with which to assess your heart. Modern heart-health monitoring technology offers incredible insights into your cardiovascular health. Wearable devices can seamlessly communicate with your smartphone and healthcare provider, providing valuable data and early warnings of potential heart issues. This cutting-edge technology is revolutionizing the way we manage and prevent heart disease. If you go to a clinic for a test and receive your results two days later, your health condition may have changed, whereas instant alerts from upcoming technologies are much more timely and accurate.

Developments in wearable tech are going to make some people very rich, and once this tech is more widely available in the mainstream, hospitals and my business will have no option but to shut down if we don't embrace the advancements, as everything will be done by AI. The AI will inform you of what medication you need, advise you of what treatment you should receive for a specific problem, and notify your regular doctor, dentist, or pharmacist if anything is wrong via an alarm system. While AI can automate many tasks, it cannot fully replicate the value of a doctor's or pharmacist's expertise. They can provide personalized advice, answer your questions, and build a trusting relationship. While technology can enhance healthcare, face-to-face interactions will continue to be an important component of your care.

I believe having both a physical and digital offering is key. Take Walmart, a brick-and-mortar company with stores all over the world, and Amazon, a digital platform selling the same products as Walmart. Eventually both companies needed to establish a physical and a digital presence to be able to serve the needs of their customers both online and in stores.

One day, in the not-so-distant future, someone is going to come out with a chip that is inserted into your body, and you won't need blood tests or doctors to do checks on you. The chip will give you real-time information about your current health conditions, so you don't need to see any medical professional in person. That real-time information will go straight to your assigned doctors and medical team, and you will see the chip will reduce medical health costs.

As someone who embraces new technology to keep my business relevant, I want to advance my technological capabilities to incorporate AI and collaborate with leaders in medical technology, as I believe it can benefit BP Healthcare Group's patients in many ways. We have already started to introduce AI into some areas of our business, and as BP Healthcare Group is very IT and tech savvy, to work for me, all my employees must be good with IT to ensure they can use and improve our systems.

The first time we dabbled in AI was in support of automation for product testing. The customer logs in and selects what tests they want to do, and payment is issued all by itself. Once we have the results, we send them, and they become available to the customer. There is also a tracking function. With this, you don't need an accounts department or anyone doing administration.

Joevy has introduced AI to eliminate the need for administration in food and environmental testing and medical waste incineration, and I no longer need the accounts department, so the accounts team has been redeployed to outlets to work on sales and marketing. In the future, nobody will need to send invoices and collect money; everything will be prepaid, just like you buy food or book an Uber. It will become the norm, and everyone will do it this way.

AI is very useful for me running a business, as to get answers from people, the turnaround time of email chains and responses can be too slow. With AI, I can get an answer immediately, but there may be some bias in the information. In the healthcare sector, the potential for AI is huge, with the possibility that it will be able to help cure diseases in the future. At the moment it is helping to screen, but to advance AI to the level of curing diseases, it will still take human input and doctors.

Legally, a decision based on AI is currently not acceptable; we still need a human touch. The future of AI will depend on the amount of data that can be captured. The more data it has, the more accurate it will be.

While AI will undoubtedly have incredible benefits not only for the provider but also for the patient, we must also be careful with it. It must only be used by people who have patients' best interests at heart. In the wrong hands, it could be very destructive.

Despite our rapid growth and advancing technology, BP Healthcare Group has stayed true to its core values as a company that cares for people. It is hard to find genuine love and care in the healthcare industry, as unfortunately many companies are motivated by making money. At BP Healthcare Group we take a humane and caring approach to our patients, and no matter how big or high tech the group becomes, this will always come first.

Laureus King Power Polo Cup, United Kingdom

Chapter 4
POSITIVE NET WORTH

My first big break came in the mid-1980s. The increase of hepatitis B in the 1980s caused a lot of concern globally, and BP Healthcare Group Clinical Laboratories stepped up to offer testing and vaccinations across Malaysia. Prior to this, I had already negotiated to decrease the cost of the test reagent substantially by buying it in bulk, enabling me to commence a large-scale hepatitis B campaign nationwide and offering massive screening and vaccination programs, which lasted many years until today and proved to be very lucrative. We had the speed, quality, and efficiency to be the first provider to offer tests and vaccines in volume and, at the best price, to make it accessible for everyone.

Because I had the network and reputation to solve problems and find solutions quickly, everyone looked to BP Healthcare Group for testing, vaccinations, and treatment for hepatitis B. Even hospital groups knew we would be able to deliver more quickly and cost efficiently than they could. The vaccine was already out there, but it had been very expensive, and only a few people could afford to take it initially. But as more suppliers started to offer it, the price came down, and it was affordable to more people.

I am a medical microbiologist, so the subjects of vaccinations, immunology, and virology are my main areas of expertise. During the hepatitis scare, I had the resources and know-how to be able to give patients confidence in our service and to answer patients' questions about the virus. I ensured that the whole of BP Healthcare Group had the skills and technology to handle the testing and vaccinations very competently, so we became the go-to option of choice for many people. As we had outlets all around the country and we had control of our own testing facilities, results, and logistics in-house, we were a one-stop center, and we could offer the quickest turnaround times by operating 24/7.

Building a Service-First Culture

Even before I started running BP Healthcare Group as my own business, when I worked for my boss in the medical testing lab, I worked 365 days per year, rapidly gaining knowledge every day. It was part of my work culture to be of service to people, and I did not take any days off. My boss often asked me if I needed days off, and I always declined. As a microbiologist, if I took even one day of leave, my results would be delayed by one day, and I would regret that I couldn't provide a superlative service with the "wow" factor. So I worked every day of the year to please my patients and ensure they were satisfied.

On my wedding day, I was supposed to pick up my wife from her family with my best man, who was also one of my key staff. That morning I called him to see where he was, and he told me to excuse him, as he had too many patients to attend to that day. He apologetically asked me to get another best man at the last minute. Thankfully,

I was able to ask a relative to stand in, and after the ceremony, we drove back from Ipoh to my hometown of Bagan Serai to meet my parents, where we went to a coffee shop restaurant for a simple lunch with some family members.

It was a very cheap and efficient wedding—just like BP Healthcare Group's services! From Bagan Serai we went to Penang Island and stayed in a beach hotel for one night. I felt a bit guilty we hadn't done more to celebrate our marriage, so I decided to book flights to Bangkok to introduce my wife to my Thai relatives there and offer prayers to some Buddhist temples in the city.

Looking back, I am remorseful we didn't have a bigger wedding celebration and invite the whole town to make my parents proud. I was the youngest child and the most highly educated and successful in my family, so it would have given them some bragging rights. My wife was also from one of the wealthiest and most prominent families in Ipoh, but she never asked for a big wedding. In hindsight it showed how much she loved me, and she cared more about being with me than an elaborate occasion. At that time, though, I was so focused on my work, and that was my main priority.

I still have the same work ethic now. If someone asks me to do something, I strive to do it to the best of my ability and as punctually as possible. This is where the experience from my early childhood, helping my parents in fruit wholesale, has helped me to be able to meet deadlines and understand tight turnaround times. If you do not meet deadlines, your perishable goods become worthless, and throwing away waste is also a wasted effort, as well as a loss of money. When it comes to healthcare, turnaround time is also paramount, and I have the natural speed and efficiency to get the best results. What's more, I keep my customers happy so they always want to come back.

If you don't have a caring character, you cannot be successful in healthcare. You must be able to serve others and not overfocus on money. I serve patients first, and the money is secondary. If they ask for a discount, I will give them a discount. Even in the early days, when I first bought the medical testing lab, every weekend I went around the country offering people free tests. By doing this I helped educate the public, and I built up a good reputation as the word about my services spread. I believe a key reason for my success and establishing a growing roster of repeat customers is building my business from a benevolent heart and earning public trust by showing my actions matched my words.

Take a large company such as Boeing, which went from being the most trustworthy aircraft manufacturer in the world to suffering a tragic downfall, and there are a lot of business lessons to be learned from this. History has repeatedly shown that if you don't keep improving your technology and you sell a product or service only to increase profit and revenue, it is a recipe for disaster. The numbers should be a by-product of a great product or service, not the main motivation. What's more, compromising on quality and cutting costs will also inevitably lead to a decline. Unlike Boeing, BP Healthcare Group's business is built on caring for customers, providing quality service, constantly trying to improve our technological processes, and making our services very user-friendly rather than being concerned about profit or high margins. We have earned faith and loyalty from patients, and we will ensure we take care of our repeat customers for life.

Everything I am doing today is rooted in caring for others and doing things right. I believe if you try to shortchange other people, or the system, by not respecting the line of the ball, this will lead to trouble. I try to live my life as simply as possible—if I am offered money to do something I don't believe is right, I won't do it. Risking bad karma is not worth any amount of money to me.

Expansion into Hospital Care

In 1991 I built my first hospital, Pantai Hospital, in Ipoh as a founding shareholder, with 285 beds. At the time in Ipoh, there were only a few private hospitals serving a population of around one million people. I secured a 3.8-acre piece of land, and the provincial governor supported me and approved the building of a new hospital there that would provide world-class healthcare services, on the condition we provided scholarships through the Perak State Foundation, which supports Perakians. First I approached the Mayo Clinic in Rochester, Minnesota, United States, to be my joint venture partner, but at that time they were not ready for international expansion. I also went to Brompton Hospital, London, and a New York City hospital. Finally I partnered with Pantai Hospital Group and built brand-new hospital facilities for Pantai Hospital Ipoh.

Pantai Hospital was highly profitable, as we developed it at just the right time when there was enough market share for us, and it was a very modern hospital. I controlled capital and operating costs and minimized unnecessary expenditure. My entry costs and investment costs were low, as the cost of the land was only RM3.4 million, and the return on investment was just four years. We always had the best technology and equipment, such as the first CT scans with sixty-four slices. It was a proud moment when we officially launched this novel CT scanner, as it was published on the front cover of *TIME* magazine that week. I announced to my CEO, "We are just in *TIME*!" and showed them the cover of the magazine. We made no compromises, but we were still able to provide services at a reasonable price and made a good margin, which was a very sustainable formula.

After twenty-seven years of ownership of the hospital, in 2018 I cashed out to Pantai Hospital Group, one of the world's biggest healthcare groups. Selling Pantai Hospital made me feel very proud and grateful, as it was satisfying that the hospital I had founded had been such a success. However, it was marked by corporate bullying and the oppression of minority shareholders, and in the end I was coerced into selling my shares, which was a bittersweet ending. After I sold it, I reinvested part of my profit into another Singapore publicly listed healthcare company, HMI, and I made another good return on investment.

Strategic Partnerships and Healthcare Innovation

At the same time in 1991, I worked with the Mayo Clinic Lab as my joint venture partner to privatize all government hospital laboratories in Malaysia with the consent of the prime minister. Mayo Clinic is the largest integrated, not-for-profit medical group practice in the world, relating to referral clinics. Dating back almost 150 years, it was established by brothers Will and Charlie Mayo, who pioneered an integrated, team-based approach to medicine. Today they treat some of the most renowned royalty, presidents, and celebrities.

Generally, I prefer not to enter into partnerships, as I like to maintain total control of my own business. But the values of Mayo Clinic Lab were very much aligned with those of BP Healthcare Group, in that both groups strive to share our knowledge and drive innovation in healthcare globally to create lasting change and better medical care for a healthier world.

We went through meetings with all the regulatory bodies and government agencies, and I proved I could confidently overcome all their concerns, but I came up against a stumbling block with the patient privacy confidentiality clause (P&C). Privatization was perceived as "pirate-ization," and P&C clauses led the government to put healthcare privatization on hold over fears of sharing patients' information and data. This was the pre-internet era, and it was very difficult to guarantee P&C would not be an issue. I was ahead of my time, as the technology solutions to overcome this didn't exist yet.

Years later we managed to outsource government healthcare services without privatization, on a cost-per-test basis, and BP Healthcare Group also started working on contracts with military hospitals, army camps, the National Heart Centre, and the General Hospital. This helped the government save more than 50 percent on costs.

BP Healthcare Group was also selected as a partner of the National Heart Institute (IJN), a specialist heart center. In our health screening business, all my doctors and specialists could help patients up to a certain point, but they often needed IJN to complete complex heart operations and treatments. So it was a mutually beneficial affiliation for both sides, as they sent their specialists to one of our centers specifically to see patients we had screened for heart problems, and we in turn could learn from their expertise. We also provided them with access to our patients, and our patients benefited from specialist services with their cardiologists.

Diversifying Beyond Healthcare

In the 1970s industrialization started to boom in Malaysia, and in 1987, together with my father-in-law, I began to invest in venture capital with a company producing rubber products. Following thirty-seven years of investment in a holding company, which operates a 260MW hydropower plant on the Mekong River along with its other diversified businesses, the dividend alone from 2003 to 2023 amounts to US$120 million, or RM500 million. However, there was a lot of underhandedness in this acquired holding company, and I have not received a single coin of dividends, as the money got lost in offshore investments. My dividends were not distributed, and every year my shares are further diluted like water through corporate exercises that benefit the other partners. One day I hope I see my money at the end of the tunnel.

Outside of BP Healthcare Group, I also invested in numerous property developments. In early 1990 I owned a 50 percent interest in 246 acres of land with my late father-in-law's partners, along the North–South Expressway, opposite the Tasek cement factory, now known as Gunung Lang Development. Subsequently, I sold my entire shareholding to my father-in-law at cost, for the simple reason it was good for my wife's family, and I already had too many things to juggle. During this time the land had appreciated from RM40,000 to RM500,000 per acre.

In 1993 I started another business development in Ipoh, where the Perak state government offered me fifteen hundred acres of land to build an integrated city. I invited a partner to help develop the land and came up with the concept to build a huge multibillion-dollar integrated development including a college, a theme park, hotels, hot springs, a hypermarket, a shopping mall, residential buildings, commercial buildings, bungalows, a resort spa, a golf driving range, and a hospital on the site. The development is now rented to different brands and companies, and thirty-two years later it is still being developed with around 200 acres yet to be built upon. My group had a 35 percent share, but the partner who owned the other 65 percent and who was in charge of construction and development engaged in fraudulent cost overruns, resulting in significant debt. This culminated in the illegal transfer of my shares without my consent or payment to me, which I reported to the police for criminal investigation, and it is still an ongoing case. This experience showed me that even publicly listed companies don't always pay or play fair.

Learning Through Challenges: Investment Lessons

In the past I've placed too much trust in people who appeared wealthy and influential, only to discover their superficiality. Given my past experiences, I'd recommend approaching business partnerships with skepticism, as appearances can be deceiving. Despite their apparent affluence, many individuals and businesses face financial difficulties caused by high debt levels. Despite their high rankings on the Forbes rich list, a significant number of individuals have negative net worth when considering their liabilities. Case in point, my partner, who is also on the Forbes list, is net negative RM10 billion (US$2.5 billion).

By the late 1990s, my investments in hospitality, industry, and property developments were giving me good financial returns and helping me have enough capital to reinvest in and expand BP Healthcare Group. Beyond my role as a medical professional running a healthcare company, I began exploring other business ventures and actively sought investment opportunities. My early venture capital investments in the 1990s yielded successful companies, and I retain founding member shares.

Over the years many people have approached me about business opportunities, collaborations, and joint ventures. As a business we evaluate the propositions we like, and I make the final decision by going with my gut instinct. Failure is usually a 90 percent likelihood, whereas success is only a 10 percent chance. You need a lot of passion, ideas, hard work, and belief to make sure any company you back will be in that exclusive 10 percent success rate. It is humbling to think that I started off needing to be financed by character funding from the bank, and now I look at business founders and decide if I like them and their companies enough to take the risk of investing in them.

The Next Generation: Environmental Healthcare

One of my most recent new ventures with BP Healthcare Group is establishing our own medical waste management and incineration company as another branch of BP Healthcare Group, which we started around three years ago. It is now operated by my son Joevy, who helps me run BP Healthcare Group, and he is very focused on growing and increasing the efficiency of this part of the business. Like Lovy, Joevy also studied and did work experience abroad but returned to Malaysia to join the family business. He started working in food and environmental testing, but I have always encouraged my children to try new businesses and have businesses of their own they are passionate about.

Medical waste incineration is a very important business, because if we did not have waste management, the earth would be toxic. People are poisoning the world. We are in this industry to help clean the world and get rid of toxic medical waste. Instead of waiting for thousands of years or more for toxic materials to disintegrate, we incinerate them, turning them into ashes that can be recycled into building materials such as cement bricks. Unfortunately many countries can't afford to do this, as incinerating in this way is a very expensive process, so toxic waste often ends up in the ocean or in landfills, but landfills are not effective or sustainable.

We had already been transporting hazardous waste since 2014, so I suggested that Joevy operate a plant, and he embarked on this new venture, securing a license that allows us to burn fifty-one tons of medical waste per day. Medical waste includes any waste that comes from hospitals and clinics, and we have all the equipment to make sure the burning is complete and goes up in the air like vapor. We have a monitor attached to the chimney that reports to the environmental department to ensure what we are outputting isn't damaging to the environment. I bought incinerators from overseas, and what started as the incineration of medical waste will be expanded to burning household waste, which becomes biomass and is converted into energy. What's more, during COVID-19, the government approved an emergency ordinance for the issuance of licenses to establish an incinerator plant to aid the government in the management of COVID-19 waste.

Financial Freedom and Future Challenges

In the 1980s and 1990s, I experienced a period of significant financial success. The BP Healthcare Group's diversified portfolio has allowed me to achieve financial freedom and enjoy an opulent lifestyle.

I'm fortunate to have built a business that generates consistent profits, enabling me to pursue personal interests such as polo and provide for my family.

In comparison to the hepatitis B outbreak in the 1980s, which was easier to control, the COVID-19 outbreak in late 2019 proved to be a much greater challenge, as it was an airborne virus transmitted through breathing, hence why it became a global pandemic. However, for all my successes up to 2019, I could never have anticipated the impact of COVID-19 and how this would create a whole new chapter in my business story.

Sultan Pahang and me

Chapter 5

THE IMPACT OF COVID-19

When COVID-19 emerged at the end of 2019, it was unprecedented. The government was initially cautious about how to manage the virus and how much money to spend on screening and immunizing against COVID-19, but they soon realized this virus was not going to be easy to stop, and it would require huge amounts of investment to control it. In my fifty years of learning about molecular technology, I had never come across anything as unpredictable as COVID-19.

COVID-19 was a key pivoting point for my business, as I was able to help the people of Malaysia during a time of global crisis, but I was also able to monetize it. It was not the first time I had offered mass screening for infectious diseases, as I was providing this in the 1980s for hepatitis B. But the hepatitis B scare wasn't as dramatic or as contagious as COVID-19. While it was large scale and gave me experience of having to provide urgent, mass volume testing and vaccinations, it was not as far spreading or unknown as COVID-19.

Hepatitis is spread through fluid, but COVID-19 is much more difficult to control, as it is passed on through breathing. The

COVID-19 outbreak was a totally different ball game compared with hepatitis B, and everyone in healthcare needed to execute faster turnaround times than we had ever been required to deliver before. For example, the collection of samples had to be quicker, as the samples were highly contagious through airborne transmission. A lot of preventative measures had to be taken, and samples had to be handled with extreme care by people wearing full personal protective equipment (PPE), including masks.

Testing for COVID-19 using molecular genomic real-time polymerase chain reaction (PCR) studies was also more time consuming and complex than testing for hepatitis B, which can be tested using a very scalable and much less costly immunology testing method. Furthermore, COVID-19 results had to be delivered faster, as there were so many samples to test, and it was critical to inform people if they had the virus as soon as possible so they could isolate and prevent further spreading. This was not the case with hepatitis B.

COVID-19 was a very divisive time. Many people suffered financially, while others profited. Some people felt trapped and depressed, while others saw it as an opportunity to reassess their life goals and plan what they would do after the pandemic. Fortunately, I was among those who benefited from the situation.

Digital Foundations and Early Response

BP Healthcare Group started off as a brick-and-mortar medical testing laboratory and clinics that patients visited for appointments. Then in 2014 the Doctor2U platform became the enabler to speed up our services and make the experience more efficient and user-friendly. These days everyone is used to accessing everything they want online—on their phones via apps—but back in 2014, we were ahead of the curve, making healthcare digital and more accessible, as no one else was doing this.

Leading up to COVID-19, I had already been growing the presence of BP Healthcare Group's physical outlets, and I had acquired a lot of properties, all of which had enough space for future expansion of services. When COVID-19 came, I already had space to conduct COVID-19 tests in isolated buildings away from my main clinics, which was important, as the virus was so infectious. Combined with my efficient IT systems, I could facilitate COVID-19 testing seamlessly. The moment we started moving, we were very far ahead of all our competitors—Garvy was on the IT side, and Joevy researched the best equipment to use.

Before COVID-19 we also had experience with H1N1 (also known as swine flu), SARS, and other airborne viral diseases that spread quickly. However, these viruses often came and disappeared within weeks, so by the time our lab ordered the test reagents, the diseases were already gone. Then came COVID-19, and we already had molecular testing machines for human papillomavirus, cancer, hepatitis C, and a few other viral studies. But at that time, those machines were only built for limited tests, and the test method took longer, as the equipment was only basic. With COVID-19, we had to introduce autosampling and robotic machines to reduce the pre-analytical time and cross infection to the handlers.

I was not really on the ball with COVID-19 until one evening, I took a phone call from my friend, who is another polo patron and the chairman of a listed company. He asked me if I had COVID-19 testing facilities, as his CEO had traveled back from overseas with another senior executive from another company. When they returned, the other gentleman fell ill and, sadly, died in the hospital. Everyone became very worried about the CEO, so I agreed to test him, and his family, staff, and everyone in his office needed testing too.

Miraculously, he did not have COVID-19, but it made me realize I had to move fast to do more tests. The next morning we started activating facilities to do more COVID-19 testing. We moved our pharmacy warehouse to different buildings and started to use spaces to create dedicated testing centers. These testing centers could not be in the same buildings as our other services, because of the risk of the infection spreading. Everyone was living in constant fear of being infectious, being infected, or unknowingly infecting others, and nobody felt safe; it was mentally tormenting.

Scaling Up Operations

When COVID-19 first broke out, I attended a government meeting in Putrajaya, Malaysia, and understandably it was clear that the government was cautious about taking the risk of spending a lot of money on the virus in case the disease lasted for only one or two weeks. If the top government officer had made the decision to spend millions on molecular testing equipment and then it disappeared as soon as it arrived, they would have been in hot water for making the wrong decision and would have been investigated for corruption and questioned why they spent millions.

However, once the severity of the virus became clear and it was certain that COVID-19 was not going to disappear anytime soon, the government had to invest multimillions of dollars to set up molecular testing facilities, even though they could only do a limited number of tests, which was not very economical.

They called in all the key players in the healthcare sector and asked who already had the molecular testing facilities they needed.

Those of us who had the required facilities and equipment were asked how many COVID-19 tests we could allocate to help the government. At the time I said I could give one thousand, and I was the biggest supporter. I went back with my son Garvy and my chief scientist, and we started ordering tests. At the start of COVID-19, we were doing only ten to twenty molecular PCR tests a day, and it took four and a half to five hours to get each test result at that time. We had to physically take the sample and put it into a tray and record it, and it was all handwritten, making it easy for mistakes to be introduced by human error. Imagine attempting to handle fifty to one hundred thousand samples and the sample sorting taking hours ... it was painfully slow and also dangerous to be exposed to the virus.

By the time I was providing one hundred thousand tests per day to the government, BP Healthcare Group's system was very quick, and once the vaccine had been created, we could also offer vaccinations. When no one else dared to invest, the government saw that BP Healthcare Group was committed to helping during the pandemic, and they knew we would give our best to fight the virus and wouldn't let our patients down. I already had healthcare outlets that could be used as screening and vaccination centers nationwide across Malaysia—no other healthcare group had this reach. So I had the network and the infrastructure, and on top of that, I was braver than anyone else. I was also running my own company, so I could make decisions quickly; I didn't need to waste time waiting for approval from anyone above me.

Innovation and Technological Advancement

Joevy started buying equipment that could improve the handling of the samples to make it safer and more efficient, as well as the software to improve the processing of results. As humans, we were very quick to adapt to COVID-19 and invent new testing equipment that could speed up the delivery of results from five hours to just forty-five minutes. At BP Healthcare Group we wanted to be the first to get our hands on the most efficient new testing solutions.

Lateral-flow tests that people can do themselves at home are not particularly accurate, but they are only used for screening, so if the result comes up positive, people would usually come to have a confirmation test done by us. Or if the result showed up as negative but the symptoms suggested otherwise, people often came for a second test with us.

At BP Healthcare Group we introduced a digital system where patients could log in and receive a barcode. Either they could come to one of our testing centers, or we could go to them at their factory or place of work. We then started a robotic system, which streamlined our testing process even further. In factories of more than ten thousand people, each person had already submitted their name and details online, so they simply arrived, gave their name, and did the swab, and the robotic system would scan their unique barcode and take the sample for testing. This saved hours of handling time for every sample. Then within twenty-four hours, the results would be sent directly to the client's phone or company system.

In airports we introduced four robotic systems that cost us millions, but everything was online, so we didn't need to do manual accounting anymore. I didn't need to send out bills or invoicing, which, again, saved a lot of time and also reduced the chance of errors in accounting.

Moving forward, Malaysia is in discussions about e-invoicing, where everything goes through this sort of system, and it also means the government gets income tax immediately. For businesspeople, it means everyone gets paid faster, so it is a very positive development.

We were the biggest COVID-19 vaccinator in Malaysia, and the government awarded BP Healthcare Group the Top Overall Outstanding Vaccination Contributor—Public-Private Partnership National COVID-19 Immunisation Programme. My late son, Chevy, also won an award for his contribution during COVID-19.

Meeting Public Health Needs

The importance of our online services became very apparent during COVID-19, serving as an enabler to reach our customers during lockdown when they couldn't visit the health centers in person. To help the most vulnerable people in need, we used national identity cards to enable students below twenty years old and senior citizens to have 50 percent discount for COVID-19 testing and some other healthcare services, and disabled people received free COVID-19 tests and healthcare. A lot of people who were struggling with a very limited income during the pandemic could also request a discount or free testing.

Other providers in the market also started to do COVID-19 testing, but many did not last, as it was very expensive. To buy the necessary molecular equipment needed to test for COVID-19, huge investment was required, and in the early days, no one knew how long COVID-19 would be around for. In the end the microbial war disrupted everyone's lives and livelihoods, lasting over two and a half years. Many businesses around the world suffered and are still suffering as a result.

Customer Service During Crisis

These days we are in a culture of complaints, especially around the timing of receiving results. During COVID-19, we received a lot of complaints from people about the waiting times for results, and it put extra strain on my staff. The customers did not realize the amount of time required to complete the tests. I asked my staff to pass all the difficult customers to me, and when their results were ready, I personally followed up with their results.

At that time there was so much panic. People were genuinely scared of dying, which caused them to be particularly anxious about getting their results. When they received their results from me, the founder and boss of BP Healthcare Group , they realized I was working very hard with my team to serve them. After receiving their results from me, they didn't complain again, as they understood BP Healthcare Group was genuinely trying very hard to help people.

Supporting National Infrastructure

The government and a large portion of the public were already using our healthcare services, so we had an existing audience, but post-COVID-19 we gained even more trust and more customers. BP Healthcare Group was asked to provide tests at airports and even for the prime minister's office. The government knew if we were asked to provide tests for emergency meetings at 8:00 a.m. the next day, with people flying in from different states needing tests to attend a meeting that morning, we would deliver for them. There were also many big companies providing essential services, such as factory production and construction, which needed tests for hundreds of thousands of people considered essential workers to keep the economy going.

For example, Malaysia is the largest producer of medical gloves worldwide, manufacturing 76 percent of the world's supply. If our glove factories had to stop producing because of staff being ill with COVID-19, it would have had a drastic impact on the rest of the world needing gloves for PPE. I really felt we had to help the whole world by keeping Malaysia's production going.

Understanding Vaccination Immunity

If you are strong, your body will produce antibodies, but of course, there are those who have weak immune systems and cannot fight the virus off themselves.

Bacterial infections are easier to treat, as you can use antibiotics. Your body has to fight off a virus, so either your own body will build up antibodies against a virus, or you need a vaccination to help fight them off faster. Many people felt they didn't have any choice about having the vaccine, as it was very complicated to travel otherwise. Of course, there were nonconformists, but for the global standard, everyone was encouraged to vaccinate, and we still continue to vaccinate children today.

Contributing to Scientific Knowledge

I did a lot of research during the pandemic and published a total of four papers on COVID-19, focusing on various methods of testing and how accurate they are compared to each other. I authored a memoir documenting my experiences with COVID-19 testing and vaccination, which was published as a hardcover book. This work serves as a historical record of the pandemic. In a study published in the *Malaysian Journal of Medical Sciences*, I explored how the pickup rate differed between vaccinated travelers from Singapore and unvaccinated travelers coming from poorer countries by observing the rate of positive COVID-19 PCR test results among inbound international travelers arriving in Malaysia via the two Kuala Lumpur international airports. I explored possible factors associated with the outcome of test results between vaccinated and unvaccinated travelers. My findings suggested that nonvaccinated travelers were 4.5 times more likely to test positive for COVID-19 compared with vaccinated travelers.

Looking to the Future

For everything we achieved in helping the Malaysian people during the pandemic, we needed to make quick decisions. At the start of it all in 2019, I remember saying to my son Garvy, "Perhaps we will make a lot of money if we are lucky." That was when I thought the virus would only last around two or three months. By 2022 we were still doing high volumes of testing, but our main aim was always to help people.

As for the future of COVID-19 and whether it will reemerge, every strain of the coronavirus constantly changes its weapons. These viruses don't just use a shotgun; they use an AK-49. We are not alone; humankind is coexisting with a microbial world and constantly battling with microbes, but we are usually the victor, as we are constantly inventing new PPE, face masks, detergents, medication, and vaccinations. Coronavirus, however, posed a big threat to us. Looking back in history, it seems that every one hundred years or so, a strain of coronavirus can wreak havoc in the human population. However, who knows if we might see another outbreak much sooner, in five or ten years' time? If it happens again, we will hopefully be more prepared.

While we are now back to living relatively "normal" lives again, we are still reminded of the COVID-19 threat, but we have a better understanding of airborne infectious diseases and preventive measures. Everyone was well educated throughout the pandemic to live responsibly and safeguard ourselves against microbial attacks.

Business Lessons and Legacy

During COVID-19, at BP Healthcare Group we realized we had a once-in-a-lifetime opportunity to maximize the capabilities of what our business could do. Our fierce competitors were bigger in revenue and market share in Malaysia before COVID-19. But during the pandemic, we overtook their pre-COVID-19 revenue, so we knew we were doing something right to surpass our competitors by so much.

Something we can take from COVID-19 for the business is that we have to stay very hungry, and we have to be focused, disciplined, and persistent in what we want to achieve. We pulled together to work as a family, and everyone in the company got involved to contribute to what we managed to accomplish in those challenging times.

Hawaii International Polo Test Match

Chapter 6

FAMILY VALUES

Family is important to me for emotional and moral support, and it is very rewarding seeing my children take an active interest in developing BP Healthcare Group, both now and in the future.

I am very family oriented. I always came home straight after work to spend time with my family rather than going out to socialize. My wife and I have now been married for over forty-five years. We still travel a lot together, and she is an unwavering source of comfort and a very calming influence on me. Post-COVID-19 we are now traveling a lot more with the whole family. Family is a pillar of support, and if I am stressed or tired after a long day, it is such a joy to return home. Building my business from scratch wasn't simple—of course, there were pressures and stresses—but I have always been focused on loving and prioritizing my family.

As I attribute most of my values and morals to the guidance I received from my mom, I have a memorial in her memory at my house in Ipoh. Among all the dos and don'ts she taught me, the most fundamental value she instilled in me was to greet others first; therefore the key family values I have tried to pass on to my children are to be humble and to greet others before others greet you, no matter who the person is or whether they are rich or poor. Garvy, in particular, applies this in his everyday life, and he even tells his friends about this value, as he feels it is very important. It is satisfying that morals from my mother have now been passed on to my children, who will pass them on to the next generation of our family.

Traditionally, the eldest son in the family would continue the throne in aristocracy and lead the company in a business empire. However, despite being the youngest of seven siblings, I have always been a natural born leader, and I became the most entrepreneurial and successful of my siblings. Perhaps because I spent more time with my mom than my siblings did, I was always learning from her indirectly. I observed that my mom had a lot of fire and determination, and she was the driving force behind my parents' business.

My children are adults now, and they all have their own plans, but when we're at home, I like us to eat together as a family before they go out. I think it's good to have this principle to maintain our family values, and my children respect it. They eat with me as a family first, then they go to see their friends.

Building Business Values in the Next Generation

I have always instilled in my children that they must work hard, give their best, go that extra mile, and be generous and humble in everything they do. My children were born into BP Healthcare Group, as I started the company before they were born. I tried to foster business sense into my children when they were growing up, and they often came to the office with me so they had a sense of what was going on in the business. Sometimes I took them with me to the bank when I went to pitch for a loan. But they also had experience working in other companies, which helped them think outside the box and bring new ideas to the way we do things at BP Healthcare Group.

One of the key business lessons I have taught my children is to act fast, as we operate in a very competitive market and have a consumer-facing business, so for every idea that is brought to the table, we need to execute it as quickly as possible. One of the main advantages of our family business is that the only person who needs to approve an idea is me, so if it makes sense for something to be implemented, with one phone call, I can give the green light to make it happen. Or I reply with my short abbreviation "GAH"—go ahead. If decisions need to be made outside the family, for example, working with a listed company, we must go through the governance of board members and directors, and often we have to wait months to get our idea discussed in a board meeting to get approval.

It is very important for them to be respected by others in their own right; therefore they are also driven to achieve things of their own, outside of the family business. I never wanted them to be complacent that they would have a job at BP Healthcare Group waiting for them, and they wouldn't have to work hard for a career. I told Lovy that her children will also have to work as hard as the rest of the family; otherwise they will be spoiled and won't develop to have a good work ethic. It is a privilege to be able to do things for others and to be respected for the work you are doing, and I am very proud of how my children are all praised and admired for their polite manners and conscientious attitude to work.

As a family we are very competitive with each other. In sports such as polo, we play together to develop our family bonding, and it also helps us be more organized in business and improves our communication and teamwork. I am fanatical about polo. After me, my late son, Chevy, was most passionate, then Joevy, Garvy, and Lovy, in order of our interest in polo. Garvy knows I like to win, even if I say I'm just playing for fun ... but there are four players in polo, and teamwork is crucial, as everyone on the field has different strengths. In business you also need to work as a team and utilize different people's strengths. In our family we all complement each other: Chevy was very good at marketing. Lovy is very good at managing human resources; Joevy is good with people skills, PR, and marketing; Garvy is good at handling government relations; and I'm good in operations, as I'm very detail oriented.

Lovy: Pioneer in Healthcare and Leadership

Lovy loved learning new things and was very curious from a young age. She has experience working in England and Singapore, and this experience has been extremely valuable, as she knows what it's like to be an employee and see things from their perspective. This is why she has always been skilled at HR and heads up the HR at BP Healthcare Group. At age fourteen she started working at BP Healthcare Group during her school holidays and on weekends.

Despite being very musical and considering pursuing a career in music (she played piano to grade eight), I encouraged her to study pharmacy instead of studying to be a medical doctor or a lawyer. Being a pharmacist is a highly recognized profession, especially in the UK, so she pursued it and didn't regret her decision. Lovy is one of the rare few blessed ones who is able to apply what she's learned in university and implement it into her pharmacy business practice compared with most of her peers. She was the pioneer and transformed pharmacy practice in Malaysia instead of waiting for the government to make a change. She believes if we want to see a change, we first have to be the change.

Lovy also joined the Malaysian Community Pharmacy Guild, a pharmacy association for the private sector. She was appointed as deputy president and also served as president for three two-year terms before becoming honorary secretary for the association. This year she was supposed to be reelected as president, but she decided to take a step back and take the role of deputy president to enable others to have a chance to rise up and lead.

When she went for an interview for an exclusive members' club, she ended up interviewing the club president. She even asked them about their five-year plan! The interviewers asked her if she had any questions, and she asked some challenging questions that put the interviewers on the spot, and they struggled to answer. She asked them straight up, "Because all of you are male, what is the female representation?" After this question, not surprisingly they wanted to wrap things up as quickly as possible. Lovy and all my children are in a different league when it comes to conducting themselves professionally. They have no fear, and they are confident, hardworking, articulate, and natural leaders.

Lovy has also taught me many things, including helping me to get up to speed with IT and digital tech. While we were in Hawaii playing polo, we visited a shopping center, where she encouraged me to buy an iPad from the Apple Store there and showed me how to use it. In a lot of Asian business families, not many of the older generation are willing to adopt digitalization, but I am very receptive to new technology, and it has helped me innovate BP Healthcare Group. As long as it adds value, reduces costs, and improves efficiency, I'm very open to bringing new technology into the business. I always try to learn from my children, staff, and other people around me and be open to change.

Lovy is bringing up her own family in the same way, which brings me a lot of joy.

Joevy: Finding His Own Path

Joevy studied economics and anthropology in school, and every summer he had the opportunity to do an internship in the finance world. His first internship was in Boston, which gave him bragging rights to say he did work experience at the Franklin Templeton Investments, a very competitive company to work for, especially as an intern. While it was a paid internship, Boston is a very expensive city, so his internship wasn't able to cover his rent for the summer. However, he found ways to save money by enrolling in night classes at Harvard summer school to earn the necessary credits, and he was also very active in networking and meeting new people.

The first year after he graduated, he was contemplating whether to go to San Francisco to do an internship or play polo, as he still had horses in England. He became attached with AIG as an intern, and they gave him an offer to work in Singapore, as they were receiving what they call a top fund and were not able to sponsor his visa. Back then he thought it might be a comfortable option, as Lovy was in Singapore, but his elder brother, Chevy, gave him a different perspective. Chevy told Joevy it is useful to work for other people to get experience, but he suggested he come back to Malaysia and work with him at BP Healthcare Group. It was essentially a choice of working for others or working for yourself. Joevy is a second-generation family member, and eventually he felt he had to come back to the family.

Chevy was like a mentor to Joevy, even when he was in college, so Joevy decided to take on the idea of working in the family, and I also helped convince him. I was approaching sixty, and I wanted to secure the future of the business. Despite this, I don't think Joevy felt any pressure; he watched Chevy work in New York for three years before returning to Malaysia. After seeing what else is out there for yourself, it is a natural instinct to want your family to be together.

I like to create some healthy sibling competition within the family. When Chevy and Joevy were working together, I encouraged Joevy not to shadow what his elder brother was doing but to try to separate ventures for himself. It is too easy for a younger brother to follow in the footsteps of his elder brother. I encouraged Joevy to try new businesses and have his own businesses, and he started a food and environmental testing lab and opened hearing testing facilities. He is now very passionate about expanding his medical waste incineration company. Being a younger sibling, you have to find your own way, and I wanted Joevy, as the third sibling, to be independent while also offering him a pathway to enter the family business.

Garvy: Entrepreneurial Spirit and Innovator

As the youngest sibling, Garvy looked up to his elder brothers and sister and started work experience at BP Healthcare Group very young. During school holidays most children of his age spent a lot of time watching TV, but in our family culture, my children started working at the BP Healthcare Group office, whether that was helping to serve patients or fetching coffees. Around the age of thirteen, Garvy helped to work in the procurement department, and he packed a lot of consumer goods, such as syringes, which needed to go to outlets.

At age fourteen he worked in the HR department, and at fifteen he worked in the marketing department, so during every school holiday, he gained experience working in different areas of the company. I made it a rule that my children started work at the same time I started, and they left at the same time I left. Some people may think this seems harsh, but it taught them how to be disciplined, and it set a good example to our employees.

Garvy has always been very entrepreneurial, perhaps because he always wanted to show he was as capable as his elder brothers and sister. When Garvy graduated in the United States in 2014, it was a natural progression for him to come back to Malaysia to work with me.

Around 2011 we were the largest employer of dietitians and nutritionists in the country after the government, and our staff were very highly regarded. If patients had any abnormalities or were out of physical shape, our professionals would provide a clear plan of action to improve their diet and nutrition, and there would be a follow-up to ensure that the patient's condition was improving.

As a by-product of this, before he graduated, Garvy set up his own restaurant business, a nutritionist-approved, healthy cafeteria located at the same site as one of our specialist centers in Ipoh. We learned that if you tell people food is healthy and will make them slim, they generally refrain from eating it, as they don't think it will taste good. Veggie outlets claiming to sell health foods are not very popular in Malaysia. But when we promoted flavorful but healthy food in our café, it did very well and gave Garvy experience in being hands on with a start-up business. It also enabled him to learn how to operate in the food and beverage sector, how to manage people, and how to negotiate the best prices with suppliers. All these skills are extremely useful in any line of business.

Following the popularity of the café, he upgraded to a French fine dining restaurant at the same locale in Ipoh and employed three French chefs. This was our contribution to introducing the people of Ipoh to fine dining and French cuisine, educating them on how food is prepared and the nuances of different cooking methods, such as sous vide and nitrogen cooking. It was poles apart from the typical local Malaysian cuisine, where people tend to eat casually and quickly before paying the bill and leaving. Fine dining is about relaxing, savoring every taste and flavor, and not rushing the experience. We often invited guest chefs, and the restaurant was always the top-rated restaurant in Ipoh on Tripadvisor.

While it was a success and a sophisticated place to socialize, the restaurant was only a sideline project to occupy Garvy while he was still at university to keep him busy and focused on his studies. I enjoyed eating at this restaurant, as I saw my friends and clients there, as well as my staff, but these days I prefer to eat at home rather than eating out.

Garvy never studied IT—he studied sociology—but he is very tech savvy and specializes in the tech and AI side of BP Healthcare Group. He reads more about these topics than I do, and he also focuses on government businesses. Over the past ten years since he joined BP Healthcare Group full time in 2014, he has been able to take a step back from operations, because the business itself has become more stable because of a streamlined IT system that has automated a lot of processes, making the group run more efficiently and providing a better service for our customers.

As the operations side was running smoothly, Garvy looked to other areas of the business that needed improving and expanding, which myself and his siblings were not already working on. He launched Doctor2U in 2014 and wanted to add further value to the company by bringing in new projects that could create more revenue and opportunities for the group following the start of COVID-19. This has included government projects and government relations, as well as working with big clients, such as airports and large corporations.

As we were very successful during COVID-19, we gained the trust of many influential people in government who saw firsthand how BP Healthcare Group can be counted on to honor our word and deliver the highest standards. Garvy is now leveraging the connections and trust we built during COVID-19 to further expand our government and corporate business.

Learning Across Generations

I used to give my children a lot of ideas of how to develop the business, but now that they are older and more experienced, they have been contributing more ideas and taking on more responsibility. This is a result of them having more exposure to the business world, reading more, and watching what our competitors and the rest of the world are doing in all industries. It is very important to look outside of the healthcare sector to see what advances are happening in other industries and how we can apply new innovations to our business.

I am now learning a lot from my children, which is vital to keep our company relevant. I come from an old school of thought—I studied microbiology fifty years ago, and we only knew about immunology to a certain level, as the technology we had then was nothing like what we have now. Molecular study has advanced, and AI is new knowledge. My children and my younger staff understand these things better and faster than I do, as they have learned about them more recently. Digitalization is also an integral area where I can learn from my children. In establishing BP Healthcare Group it's like I have built the brick-and-mortar part of the house, and now the younger generation is helping me digitize it.

I know my children respect what I have created, giving them a platform they can build on to grow further. The hardest part was setting up the foundations over forty-five years ago, and my children are grateful I did this.

In Memory of Chevy

My late son, Chevy, and I spent a lot of time together, and he always aspired to achieve more than me. Wherever he failed to do better than me, he felt disappointed in himself. I miss him a lot, as wherever he went, he liked me to accompany him. Whether it was visiting him at school and university in England and America, or watching him play polo tournaments around the world, he always asked me to come along. Chevy had a very special personality, and he wanted me, his father, to be around so we could enjoy and experience things together. He also exposed me to many new parts of the world that I wouldn't have discovered otherwise.

No matter how tired or busy he was, he would always go back to Ipoh on the weekend to see his mom, spend time with his family, and ride our horses there. He was equally as obsessed with polo as I am. I am devastated he had to leave this world earlier than me and so soon after his marriage. He had a fantastic education, and he loved his studies. He studied in Malaysia and England, then he went to Stanford, Peking University, and Harvard before studying at the University of Virginia. He worked as an investment banker in New York and as a qualified chartered alternative investment analyst. He excelled academically, and while his brothers both achieved a five-goal polo handicap, he was not far behind with four goals. He won the

American National Intercollegiate All-Star Award, and his name is in the Museum of Polo and Hall of Fame in Florida, United States.

Chevy loved polo, and I will continue to play for the Dato Chevy Beh Memorial Cup, which is now a tradition hosted by La Dolfina Polo in Argentina as a tribute to Chevy. The day is dedicated to commemorating his life, with a polo match including some of the world's greatest ten-goal players showing their respect and gratitude, such as Poroto Cambiaso, David Stirling, Adolfo Cambiaso, and Diego Cavanagh. It is an opportunity to bring together family and friends in Chevy's honor and to reflect on the exceptional person he was and the impact he had on all those who met him.

Chevy was a Forbes Healthcare contributor for Asia, and he connected me with the Forbes family and pushed me to write this book. For me, writing a book is like taking on another job but not making money from it. So I started this project about four years ago but lost momentum. Then when Chevy passed away, I took the opportunity to reignite this book in his memory, as I know he was proud of me and wanted to push me to tell my story. He was a go-getter, working in the office seven days a week like me. He was the first of my four children to return home and work with me after he graduated and worked in New York for two years. He made a big contribution to the expansion and improvement of BP Healthcare Group's services, and he helped me grow the company through advertising and publicity, as this was something he really believed in. He looked at big brands such as L'Oréal, which had been very successful during the economic downturn, and he used them as an example of how to push branding and marketing, implementing similar strategies at BP Healthcare Group.

Following his experience working in one of the biggest special purpose acquisition companies in New York, a publicly traded company created for the purpose of acquiring or merging with an existing company, he continued to work in this sector when he returned to Malaysia. Subsequently, after a couple of years, Malaysia started to introduce special purpose acquisition companies, and we decided to revisit this with a company we named Asian Healthcare Group. Then Chevy left BP Healthcare Group to work on a new venture, but sadly it was not successful. In hindsight it was actually for the best it didn't work out, as at that time, valuation was very high. If it had been successful, he would have bought very expensive healthcare businesses, and it would have been even more difficult to make money. I helped him make up the losses, as he was never irresponsible with money—he never used money to gamble or in the wrong way; he was just trying to seek his fortune. I am very proud of him, as he tried hard to make his investments work.

Later, he set up BookDoc company, a platform to help all healthcare players get closer to their customers. This was only a small company, as the population of Malaysia is small. To create a huge company, you have to be a business such as Google or Microsoft, with the world's population as your audience.

Then the pandemic came, and during this time Chevy worked in parallel with me on vaccinations and COVID-19 testing on a large scale, which gave him a large profit. He was financially secure at the time of his passing. As a father, I am trying to work out how to return the money to his trusted investors, as many of our friends believed in him and invested in him, but unfortunately it is not that simple.

He should have continued enjoying his wonderful life. Shortly after he passed away, he was due to fly to Aspen to play in a charity polo game with Prince Harry. During that game Prince Harry respectfully held a minute of silence for Chevy. During the dinner Prince

Harry made a speech paying tribute to Chevy, along with fellow polo players Nacho Figueras and Malcolm Borwick.

Chevy was very well connected at university, and he built good friendships wherever he went. Indeed, his interest in networking and making friends made Joevy's and Garvy's lives easier, as Chevy had already established many connections for them.

He also established many collaborations and built good relationships with higher-education establishments to promote our company. After studying abroad and gaining lots of life experience, he knew things I didn't know about how to scale the business.

Legacy and Succession

Thinking ahead, I sometimes wonder if my children will sustain the same interest in the company as I have. Perhaps, if they are alone without spouses, they may focus on the business. However, if they get married, they might have other foci. If they don't have an interest in continuing the company legacy, the company will fail. The company has offered my children a world of opportunities, from attending global events to achieving professional success and financial stability. Despite their accomplishments, they continue to be humble and respectful toward others.

I thought I had my life and my family's future all planned out. Then when Chevy passed away, I had to rethink those plans. I had given each of my children ownership and responsibility of a specific business unit of their own, to incentivize them to run and manage their own business successfully. The other siblings also had a smaller share in each of these businesses. The thinking behind the distribution of shares was that if the sibling with the greatest share did well, the other siblings would also benefit. Yet if they wanted to be more independent, their small shares in their siblings' companies could be bought out and vice versa. Both Chevy and Joevy not only successfully ran their own departments of BP Healthcare Group, but they also started their own businesses and ventures outside of BP Healthcare Group, branching out and achieving success beyond the family business.

My wife always said not to distribute anything to our children until I pass. But I wanted to give them enough to "try out" so I could see how responsible they were with their wealth. All of them have proved they work hard and are very financially responsible, so I am not worried about how my children will handle their finances in the future. Ultimately we can make plans, but God will decide the outcome.

When Chevy passed away, I felt my formula had failed. But as often happens in life, things don't always turn out as you expect. Perhaps God has made things turn out this way to make me rethink some things in my life. My son Joevy said to me, "Dad, maybe we didn't do enough good things." And maybe he is right, but we can only keep trying to do the best we can.

Looking After Our Extended BP Healthcare Group Family

Now that my children are established, I am more focused on looking after my key staff when they reach retirement age. I have even told my children, if anything happens to me, those who have served me well over the years need to be taken care of. Our employees know if they work hard for us, they will be rewarded with a generous golden handshake, which is tax-free in Malaysia.

Two groups of my long-standing staff who have gone above and beyond and who have shown sustained commitment and loyalty have already been given the golden handshake. The first team to receive the golden handshake and other benefits such as scholarships for their whole families and nice cars had been working for me for over thirty years. The second team who have been working for me for around fifteen years are already starting to receive benefits as well. And I am now starting to reward the third group, who have been working with me for around ten years.

Continuing the Family Legacy

BP Healthcare Group's success and growth can be attributed to our commitment to cost-effective practices, efficient operations, and a dedicated team of employees and suppliers who share our vision and values. It all comes down to trust, and it has not always been straightforward, but through word of mouth and some advertising overseen by Chevy, we have built up a very good brand reputation.

My children are also very active in networking and attending conferences, and everyone who knows our family always praises me for how well my children conduct and articulate themselves. This is something they learned from schools in England, where they were taught how to be polite. These days my children are more polished in PR situations than me, so often, they go out and network and fly the flag for BP Healthcare Group, and I stay more behind the scenes. My children's generation is all about being PR savvy, so I leave it to them.

But a lot of the respect and trust BP Healthcare Group has gained has been because of the trust and respect people have had in me and all the work I have put in over the years. So it is still important for me to show up and be seen and to keep up relationships I have been nurturing.

I don't see myself retiring anytime soon, and I still generally go to bed at around 10:00 p.m. and wake up at 2:00 or 3:00 a.m. to start working. But I would like my children to run the operations side of things. I want to keep expanding, not only BP Healthcare Group but also some of my early investments that are also very successful. I often have people offering to buy the BP Healthcare Group, and I ask my children if they would like to sell it. But they question, What are we going to do with ourselves if we have more money but no business to run? When you don't have a company to focus on, you start creating problems in your head, but when you have a business to run, you wake up energized every day. There are so many decisions to make or issues to solve.

I feel proud when I wake up in the morning and people are waiting for my instruction. It makes my life exciting, and it makes our family life interesting too.

Donation of the Beh House, Virginia

Chapter 7
GIVING BACK

I believe that those who are fortunate enough to achieve financial success have a duty to give back. My commitment to charitable causes is a reflection of my values, and it has earned me recognition in the polo community and beyond. My commitment to supporting charitable causes and community service has earned me respect in the polo world and beyond.

I have donated generously to charity over the years, but I have not just given in monetary value; I have also given a lot in kind, such as offering free health tests, services, and discounts to people who cannot afford them.

I like to give to genuine charities who approach me after devastating natural disasters such as floods, and I often put an extra "0" on the end of whatever figure the charity has requested. Helping people who are desperately in need gives me inner peace and satisfaction.

Supporting Sports and Charities

Supporting sports in Malaysia is also something I am passionate about, such as badminton, one of the sports in which we can reach world standards in Malaysia. During COVID-19, a number of big corporations suffered, and the Badminton Association of Malaysia and Olympic Council of Malaysia came to me for support, and I donated the amount of money they requested.

I have been donating to the Laureus Sport for Good Foundation for more than seven years now, an organization devoted to supporting the power of sport and sporting excellence to spread good around the world. The first patron of Laureus was Nelson Mandela, who said, "Sport has the power to change the world. It has the power to unite people in a way that little else does. Sport can awaken hope where there was previously only despair."

I wholeheartedly agree, and I will always remember an American Peace Corps volunteer who used to come to my school in Bagan Serai and give his time to teach us how to play baseball in the evenings. He was very humble, always wore a T-shirt with Wisconsin written on it, and rode a bicycle everywhere. His selflessness and generosity in sharing his time and expertise to teach us a new sport had a profound impact on me, and as an adult I wanted to find my own way of giving a similar experience back to others.

I choose to donate to the Laureus Foundation, as it uses sport to help children and disadvantaged people all around the world and raises funds from various charity sporting events each year. Using the money that is raised, the organization sends famous athletes to remote and often disadvantaged areas to teach people sports. This gives those with limited resources a chance to learn new skills and discover unknown talents—perhaps even becoming superstars themselves—and using the spirit of sport to bring improvements to their whole town.

Contributions to Polo and the Community

I started giving to charities before I was thirty years old when I donated a building for a hospital in my father's name, Beh Heng Boey. In Argentina, the Pieres family asked me to contribute to a charity to help polo grooms from disadvantaged backgrounds have a place to spend downtime in Pilar, a city around one hour drive from Buenos Aires, where there are many polo facilities, but outside of the polo bubble, the area is very poor. Instead of relying on multiple donors, I decided to personally fund the project. As a gesture of gratitude, "Beh House" was named in my honor.

In America I was asked by the University of Virginia to make a large donation for a university building, so another Beh House was built. Now when the United States Polo Association (USPA) goes to Virginia for a national meeting, they hold it in Beh House. The building also provides players and visitors much-needed accommodation and a place to rest.

I have been a big supporter of the Royal Charity Polo Cup at the prestigious Guards Polo Club over the years. The charity tournament is always played in an exciting round robin format, usually with the Duke and Duchess of Cambridge in attendance, and HRH Prince William, the Prince of Wales, plays on one of the teams. It is always a very special occasion to play with members of the royal family and to have a photo with them after the games. BP Healthcare Group Polo Team has played in the charity tournament for a number of years, contributing to charities supported by TRH the Prince and

Princess of Wales, including MHI (Shout), Wales Air Ambulance, Centrepoint, the Passage, Mountain Rescue England and Wales, Foundling Museum, Forward Trust, East Anglia's Children's Hospices, Baby Basics, Little Village, and Abernecessities.

In 2024 Lovy played in the Royal Charity tournament for the first time, as in previous years, she has been pregnant and unable to play. It was particularly special for her to play alongside Prince William, and it was serendipitous that the tournament was played on July 12, as it coincided with her daughter's birthday. It turned out to be such a memorable day, as Prince William wished my granddaughter happy birthday with a handshake and a high five.

As a long-standing trustee, I also continue to support and donate to the Boy Scouts. This organization is close to my heart, as it gave me so much purpose and joy as a child and young adult. I am now very happy to be able to give back to the Scouts and help it continue its inspiring work with young people. While giving to the community is a vital part of my philosophy, I also believe that charity begins at home—with the people who work alongside me every day. Supporting my staff is just as important as giving to society at large, as they are the backbone of everything I have built.

Giving Back to My Staff

I am now at a phase in my life where I want to give back to my staff in the same way I have provided for my family. When I leave this world, I wish for all my staff to remember how I helped them improve their lifestyle and financial standing. I believe in charity at home first, then I can look to charity outside.

My staff rely on me in some ways, and I am dedicated to providing them with the opportunities and support they need to build successful careers to improve their lifestyle standards. I have everything I need in life, but I want BP Healthcare Group to continue growing to keep helping my staff and for my patients and customers to be happy.

When I started my first job working for my boss, I was able to stay with one of his brothers in his family home, so I didn't have to pay rent for lodgings. At the beginning of my career, this was a huge help to me while I was finding my feet, and it made me realize the importance of ensuring all my staff have a place to call home and don't have to worry about accommodation when they start working for me.

For new graduates who come to work for me from the outskirts of the city, I have a building near the office that provides free accommodation for them for the first six months, until they are financially stable. This means they can be focused on their work and don't have to worry about money or where they are going to live when they first start work, as uncertainty about living arrangements can cause a lot of stress.

Under my management, I always give everyone an incentive to work hard, as the company rewards employees for every extra thing they do and any overtime they put in. I want to show my appreciation to the people who work hard for me, and in my BP Healthcare Group culture, people who work closely with me can feel I am grateful for every effort they make. This means for every task they receive, they will do the best they can, which is beneficial for the company overall.

I spend a lot of time developing relationships with my staff so they know I care for them, and I genuinely want to help them out. I tell them if they need any financial help, they can come to me. For example, one of my polo staff asked to borrow money from me to buy a new car. I just gave him the money, as I didn't want him to be in debt to me. It was a small gesture on my part, but for him, being able to buy a car was life changing.

Growing up, I was the youngest in my family, and all my siblings are above seventy years old now and retired. I still have good relationships with them, and one of my brothers who used to help me in the company is still involved. We call him "Papa Auditor," meaning he is highly experienced and wise. He takes trips around the country to advise on which BP Healthcare Group outlets need to improve and when outlets need renovations. I need the knowledge of "papa auditors" to teach my younger staff. Education and learning should always be a nonstop process, and less experienced staff can learn from people who have worked for me for a long time.

With any big company, you cannot build it and then expect it to run by itself. Today some of my staff have been working for me for more than forty years. But in the younger generation, we have a big turnaround of staff. These days younger people often feel entitled to jobs and are either not willing to stick at it or think there are better options out there. My approach to supporting my staff stems from my broader philosophy on leadership and career growth. Just as I value loyalty and hard work in my team, I believe these principles have been the foundation of my own success and are essential lessons for any aspiring leader.

The Value of Loyalty and Career Progression

For me, making frequent job changes to add to your CV is the wrong way of progressing your career. I believe it is better to demonstrate loyalty and continuity with one company, where you can potentially grow to the top of that company and become a shareholder. Or you could even buy the company and become the owner, as I did. Whenever I see any staff who are interested in joining BP Healthcare

Group, we look at the number of years they've been working and how many companies they have moved around. The likelihood is that if someone has worked for lots of different companies already, they are not likely to be employed to be a future leader in my company. There is no point putting a lot of time and effort into developing them if they are going to leap off like a grasshopper at the next opportunity.

If someone comes to me who has worked for the same company for a long period and then the company relocates and they don't want to move, this is a valid reason to look for a new job. Ideally I like to employ new graduates straight out of university, as they are more malleable to work with, and I can offer them a long-term career path.

The Business Tree Analogy

As I have said before, a business is like a tree—the most important components are the roots, the trunk, and a few main branches. The leaves can come and go, but the roots and the trunk must stay strong. The leaves are like staff, and in the business world, a turnover of staff of between 10 and 30 percent is acceptable. One leaf can fall in winter, and another will grow in spring. Money is like fertilizer—the more of it you put on the trees, the more the trees grow. The more you invest into your business and your staff, the more you will profit.

When it comes to manpower and retaining and repaying good staff, of course, the number one factor is money. Without good money to pay, you won't get good staff, and if you don't have good staff, your services will deteriorate. However, I believe strongly in empowering my existing and new staff with knowledge and training to give them the chance to progress and rise within the company. It is not just about giving them a salary every year. When you create opportunities in your business, good staff who are ambitious will want to help you capitalize.

We have also formed collaborations with top universities around the world such as Universiti Sains Malaysia, Universiti Malaya (UM), Universiti Kebangsaan Malaysia, and the University of Nottingham, among many others. I used to run my company in a small way, but as you grow and become a national player, you have to play your role as a good Malaysian citizen and give back to society. Rather than keep trade secrets, we have opened up to universities so they can come to us, and we can help each other to continue increasing our knowledge and research and support the training of the next generation of talent in the healthcare industry.

Balancing Kindness and Leadership

Many people think the youth of today are like a totally different species, but we should not generalize that all the younger generation are disparate from the older generation. Often, the younger generation still has a similar mindset to the older generation's way of thinking, but now they have access to more opportunities.

Humans are the same, regardless of race, color, or religion. Therefore operations are all about psychology, dealing with human beings and how to take care of their interests. However, this is a balancing act, because if you are too kind, it can be seen as a weakness. I often find myself being too kind.

Some people who work for me stand out, as I can see the teaching from their families has given them good foundations, and I am very thankful to have people with strong family values working in my company. I always tell them to go home and tell their parents the boss says congratulations for bringing them up so well.

Reflections on Success and Responsibility

My mom always told me if I worked for other people, I needed to make sure the boss loves me. That meant doing the best I could for my company, respecting my boss, and giving everything I could to help make the company successful. This is how I was brought up.

I hardly caused trouble for my parents, even when I was left unsupervised. As the youngest, I always wanted to impress them. Everything my siblings could do, I wanted to do, too, and when my parents gave me responsibility and trusted me to do the work, it gave me a great feeling of satisfaction, so I completed it to the best of my ability.

I only worked for my first boss for just over a year, and I had already made the company more profitable. It was because he saw how passionate and hardworking I was that he asked if I would buy the company. And this was only my first job! If you are focused and talented, you can progress from an entry-level job to chairmanship. If you are easily distracted and not willing to commit yourself, you will be job hopping, and in that case, it is you that is the problem, not the employer. I employ staff as I need their services and because they can help cover certain job responsibilities. I take pride in looking after my staff, but I am not a welfare home, so people don't come to work for me to just turn up and get paid. They must earn it.

Financial success can sometimes lead to increased expectations from others. In the past, when the company faced financial challenges, my employees were understanding and supportive. However, as the company's fortunes improved, some employees became more demanding and less willing to tolerate delays in salary payments. While I'm always willing to assist employees in need, I've encountered instances where advance payments have been misused, whereby some employees went missing in action. I really hope that the government can support employers to help break bad habits, as it can ultimately be cancerous.

After a few months of working in my first job, I bought a second-hand Toyota Corolla from my brother-in-law, who had upgraded his car following a promotion. Rather than pay for the car outright, he gave me an interest-free repayment plan over two years, which made the ownership of my first car easy, as I didn't need to make a down payment for the car.

Ever since I was in high school in Ipoh, when I saw nice cars drive past, I aspired to have a luxury car in the future. Indeed, it is every young boy's dream to have an amazing car. After my modest Toyota, I upgraded to a BMW 320, which was first introduced in Malaysia in 1983. BMW had just started exporting its cars to Malaysia, so you didn't see many BMWs around at that time. My first brand-new sports car was a Porsche 944, which I bought in the 1980s, when I was increasing my wealth during the hepatitis B screening rollout. In the past forty years or so, I have indulged my passion for cars, and I now have a fleet of luxury supercars.

Certain cars are seen as a mark of achievement. When you make money, the first thing you wanted to do in those days was buy a car. The scale goes like this: Your first car only needs to get you from A to B, your second car will be an upgrade, and you will also get a Rolex. Then you keep upgrading your car to more sporty and luxurious models until you realize you have too many cars, and they become a burden. You also buy more Rolex and Patek Philippe watches for you and your wife. But when you have too many, you don't wear any, and you don't need any more. It becomes like that with all material possessions and property.

This is why my life is not so much about the money and what it can buy; instead it is about being happy; spending time with my family, my company, and my staff; enjoying playing polo; and traveling. I also want to make sure all my children are self-made, successful entrepreneurs so they can enjoy reaping the fruits of their labor and be able to give back to others too. When you're living a good life and helping other people, I believe you should also enjoy yourself and not feel bad for spending money on yourself as long as you are also giving back.

At the time of writing, I am sixty-eight years old, and I am incredibly grateful for what I have achieved in my life. I now own more assets than I ever dreamed of. But I have come to realize the more assets I have, the more stress and headaches they bring, as managing a lot of assets and properties comes with a lot of problems.

One thing my son Garvy said to me that I will never forget is that as we gain more wealth in life, and we attain the things we always aspired to and more, such as enough polo horses to enable the family to play competitively, the more problems we have. Whether it is a problem with a horse or a problem with a car or a property, there is always something that needs fixing or addressing. With the current global trend, having enough manpower for the maintenance of all these possessions is a constant mental harassment.

I am now facing self-inflicted problems. People look at me and envy my lifestyle. But they don't realize how much hassle I have every day managing all these things. Once you achieve what you really aimed for in life and you buy the things you had always dreamed of owning, you still have to stay motivated, which is why you have to keep setting more goals and setting yourself new challenges.

Every time I achieve what I set out to accomplish and when the business is stable, I get bored. Every time I get bored, sales go stagnant, so we are always creating something new to improve or expand our business. I always need to keep challenging myself to keep things exciting. Perhaps that's because I was born in the year of the monkey—monkeys find it impossible to sit still!

Dr. Beh Chun Chuan and his son with the best polo player in the world, Adolfo Cambiaso. Two-generation polo family competing in Sotogrande, Spain

Chapter 8

PASSION FOR POLO

In many ways I have been guided by my passion for polo and the philosophy of following the line of the ball. In polo staying on the line is about precision, discipline, and seizing opportunities—principles that extend to how I approach business and life. Just as crossing the line in polo disrupts the game and causes chaos, deviating from your path in business can lead to missteps and setbacks. Polo and business both take dedication and drive. If you aim to play polo well, you must be passionate. If you don't have passion in business, you won't be successful. Playing polo and running a business both require a lot of transferable skills and attributes.

Learning to Ride and Embracing Polo

I began playing polo in Ipoh in the late 1980s, when I was invited by a customer to support a debilitating old polo club there. Ipoh is one of the wealthiest cities in Malaysia, because it was the largest producer of tin in the world, and it has attracted a lot of expats since the early

1900s. The story of the first polo club in Ipoh is that it was founded over 150 years ago by Sultan Iskandar of Perak.

My family and I had no prior experience with horses, so I started off taking riding lessons with Lovy and Chevy, and soon we all got hooked on riding. It is perhaps no coincidence that my surname, Beh (马), means "horse" in Chinese. I did some research tracing back the origins of our family name, and we discovered in the northwestern region of China, there were many horsemen and warriors, and the emperor respected us as loyal and committed army cavalrymen. Our ancestors were from the Mahmud and Muhamad tribes, which may explain why we have an inherent affinity for horsemanship.

I was not a horse rider to begin with, however, and if there is one key lesson learning to play polo taught me in the early days, it is if you fall off the horse, you have to get back on and keep trying, no matter how many times you fall. I only spent two weeks learning how to ride before I started polo, as the polo club didn't have enough players, so I was thrown in at the deep end, and I fell off a lot in the beginning.

But life is not about trying not to fall off and avoiding taking any risks. It is about trying, falling off, trying again, falling off again, and keeping getting back on the horse every time you have a setback. And each time I got back on the horse, I found a clearer path forward—just like in polo, where staying on the line of the ball keeps you moving toward your goal. Falling off, in life or in polo, doesn't matter as much as having the determination to follow the right path.

Despite being a very difficult and dangerous sport to learn, many people actually take up learning to play polo later in life, and many of them are not experienced horse riders. You can be taught how to ride and play polo at the same time, and sometimes this is an advantage. Many people who come to polo with a riding background in other equestrian disciplines such as dressage or show jumping often struggle to adapt to the polo technique, as it is a very counterintuitive way of riding to what they are used to.

The Rules of Polo and Business

The rules of polo are complicated, but there is a fundamental rule that is very important for keeping the game flowing and preventing injury to yourself, the horses, and other players. If spectators know this rule as well, it also helps them enjoy the game more and understand what has happened when umpires blow their whistles for a foul during a fast-paced game.

The main rule of polo—and the most common foul that is committed—is not crossing the line of the ball. The line of the ball is created when a player pursuing the ball is given a clear path ahead, and no other players can cross this imaginary line to try to steal the ball for themselves. Crossing the line once the ball has been played is extremely dangerous, and just like doing the wrong thing in business could cause serious implications, making the wrong move in polo is extremely risky and could lead to injury, or worse.

This is why in life and business, as in polo, you must follow the line of the ball and play within the rules. Once you have your line, you must pursue it, and others must respect your right-of-way. Likewise, you must also respect it when others have the line, you can only follow closely behind and take a chance to hit the ball if those in front of you miss it. If the ball is missed, you must be ready to seize the opportunity, making split-second decisions as the game changes. On the polo field or in business, you can't conduct yourself ruthlessly, lawlessly, or unethically; you must do things morally, consciously, and legally in the right way.

From Ipoh to Argentina

After starting to learn polo with Lovy and Chevy, my other two sons, Joevy and Garvy, also joined in, and we became a family polo team. I built my own polo facility in Ipoh, with stables, a polo field, and turnout for the horses. My house backs right onto the polo field with a spectacular view of the surrounding mountains. I always have Argentine grooms and players at home in Ipoh to play polo practices with us and to help care for the horses and keep them fit and prepared to play in tournaments.

Once I learned the basics of polo in Ipoh, I told myself I needed to improve my polo and reach a higher level, so in the late 1980s, I went to Argentina, the beating heart of polo. Polo is a national sport in Argentina comparable to football, and I already had some business interests in the country, so I started spending time there and used it as an opportunity to invest in my polo training. Argentina is home to the highest level of polo in the world, and the Argentina Open polo tournament in Palermo, Buenos Aires, is the pinnacle of the polo calendar each year, seeing the best polo players in the world (often all Argentines) battle it out for the coveted trophy.

It was in Argentina where I sought the most respected people to teach me to play and where I first met the greatest polo player in the world, Adolfo Cambiaso, who was only a young boy at that time. Salvador Socas, Cambiaso's half brother, was my first polo teacher over thirty years ago, so I know their whole family very well. Over the years I have had the privilege of playing with Cambiaso in England, Spain, and Argentina.

I have learned a huge amount playing with Cambiaso, and the best advice he gave me is, first, "Don't call for the ball. Before I touch the ball, I already know where you are, so run discreetly, and I'll send the ball to you." And second, "Be patient. When you're not patient, you create a foul. When you are patient, the other team will become impatient and cause the fouls." This is another level of polo skill and intuition.

Playing at the Highest Level

I have played polo at all levels, from low goal to high goal, but playing in the San Jorge Open, a thirty-two-goal tournament in Palermo, Argentina, with some of the best players of the world, was an incredible and nerve-racking experience. In the San Jorge Open, every move was critical, and following the line of the ball meant maintaining focus under immense pressure. Just as in business, where navigating competitive markets demands precision, playing at this level required staying true to my strategy while adapting to rapid changes on the field. I had played with Cambiaso and other top-rated players in England and Spain, but in Palermo the level of competition is on another level.

Indeed, there is nowhere quite like field one and field two in Palermo, Buenos Aires, named by those in the polo world as the "Cathedral of Polo." The world's most famous polo grounds are surrounded by imposing high-rise buildings; it is quite surreal to play there, located in the middle of a metropolis, and the atmosphere is electric. All my four children had played in Palermo, and I was the only one who hadn't played there until 2021, when I was sixty-five. It was one of my bucket list goals, which I am very proud to have ticked off my list. What made the experience even more special was having the opportunity to play against my son Joevy, who was on a different team.

Despite being sixty-five years of age at the time, I played two games in Palermo and scored a total of ten goals. At this age such a performance is extremely satisfying. Even at thirty-two-goal level at top speed, any ball that is sent to me, I can put in the goal. Adolfo Cambiaso, a renowned polo player, admires my hitting accuracy and particularly my under-the-neck shot, which I learned from his half brother.

I am sixty-eight this year, and while I have now stopped playing competitive tournaments, as long as my health is good and I'm physically fit, I'll continue to play social polo. I still have many horses, so I can't give up immediately even if I wanted to. My sons continue to excel at polo, and now my young grandson, Lovy's son, is beginning to learn how to ride. We plan to introduce him to the sport of polo as soon as he is ready, to see if he develops a passion for it. As I pass down the love for polo to my children and grandson, I hope they will learn not just to play but also to follow the line of the ball in all aspects of their lives. Staying true to their path, respecting others, and seizing opportunities are lessons that polo—and life—teach us.

If I feel I'm out of the game, I don't want to play. I like to actively contribute and score good goals. At last year's Queen's Cup, they highlighted five of the best goals in the tournament on social media, and one of them was mine. I generally score quite a lot of goals in high goal tournaments, but currently I hope my handicap remains zero in consideration of my advanced age. These days I just like to play chukkas, and I'm happy if I score a few goals. I don't need to play competitive tournaments anymore; I just want to play for fun.

The handicap system in polo ranges from minus two to ten goals, with a minus two handicap given to the lowest-level players and a ten-goal handicap awarded to the highest-level professional players in the world. To put a team together, the combined handicaps of the four players on each team must match the other teams, depending on the level of the tournament. For example, in a high-goal, twenty-two-goal tournament in the UK, the combined handicap of each team must add up to twenty-two goals, so a team could be made up of a zero-goal player (the patron), a five-goal player, a seven-goal player, and a ten-goal player.

Patrons fund the team, and most patrons and amateurs do not play with more than a two-goal handicap, and playing as a one- or two-goal rated amateur is considered an impressive feat. My sons Joevy and Garvy have both achieved five-goal handicaps as amateurs, and at a recent handicap review, they were proposing moving them up to six goals. If they had focused only on polo, I am sure they could have reached the highest handicaps, but at six goals we are preparing for them to play in the Argentina Open.

When I was interviewed twenty-five years ago and asked what my dream was in polo, I said it was to see my children play in the Cámara de Diputados Cup. Now they've played in the Cámara, and six goals is the minimum handicap to play in the Argentina Open; everything is possible. We will find a way to set up a team so they can play in the open. All my children want to surpass me. And I have made my standards very high! But while Joevy and Garvy have the potential to play at the pinnacle of the sport, they also know their limitations in polo, and business is their main priority. They are never going to play polo professionally.

One of my polo ponies is currently being played by Adolfo Cambiaso and was played at the Argentina Open in 2024 with him. She is a six-year-old mare named Alberta Augusta, and I am still the owner, but I lent her to Cambiaso, as he can make her a famous horse.

He played her in one chukka, and afterward he was like an excited toddler who wanted a new toy!

She is a very special horse, and anyone can play her and score a few goals on her, but Cambiaso made her exceptional.

He was losing a game by five goals, and when this horse went into the game, Cambiaso changed the dynamic of the game by scoring five goals to equalize.

If you run a family organization like mine, polo is a wonderful sport to help train your children to be good in business. But there is also a danger that if they get too immersed in polo, they will not concentrate on their day jobs. My children have been very lucky; they have been able to play a very good level of polo and to be exposed to some of the best polo players in the world from a young age. They were already playing high-goal polo when they were around fourteen years old. I was once asked if I worried about the danger of my children playing polo, and I didn't answer. I am even more fanatical about polo than my children! Even as children they knew how to read the game and stay out of trouble, and they knew how to ride in a way that minimizes their risks of having an accident.

The downside of getting better at polo as an amateur means that sometimes professionals play dangerously against you, because they know you are a strong enough rider to take it. But my children and I know when to put on the brakes and pull the horse up to save ourselves rather than getting into a battle that could result in an injury, or worse. We know we have too much to lose. All this experience in polo has helped my children to mature faster. It is the best kind of active learning—polo is a complex sport that requires so many qualities, including focus, resilience, determination, precision, strength, and stamina.

In general, it is very difficult for non-Argentines to make it as top players with seven-, eight-, nine-, or ten-goal handicaps, as Argentina is the epicenter of polo pony breeding, polo facilities, and polo family dynasties. Tommy Beresford is perhaps the only English player currently coming close to competing with the Argentines (although he is half Chilean). But for patrons to reach this level playing only for fun, it is even harder.

I have never seen a patron play as well as Fred Mannix, who reached a nine-goal handicap at his peak. He is an idol for our family, as he is an excellent player and patron, and he also has a successful breeding and training program for polo ponies called Alegria. My son Garvy played with him for the Commonwealth Team against the England team at the Coronation Cup at Guards Polo Club in 2023, and Garvy made history as the first Malaysian player to play in this historic tournament. Despite not winning the match, the Commonwealth Team put up a very strong performance.

Two generations of renowned polo families: Beh and Adolfo Cambiaso

Lessons beyond the Polo Field

After playing polo for thirty years, I am still learning from the game. And when you play polo at a high level with the best players in the world, your polo organization becomes a business in itself. I have tried to use polo to teach my children practical experience and management skills that prove to be invaluable to them in the business world. Polo has taught my children and me to think flexibly and master complex coordination skills. It's also shown us that even perfect teamwork doesn't guarantee victory when facing a superior opponent.

Dealing with the polo industry can certainly be tricky. Now my children are grown-up, and when we talk about business, we talk about it like a polo game. Just like running a successful company, polo requires leadership skills, teamwork, strategy, and quick decision-making. As it is a high-risk, dangerous sport, it is important to be fully prepared, as you are not only responsible for your teammates but also your horses.

At the top level of polo, it is a huge organization like running a business, but there is no return on investment. If I spent the same amount of time on my business as playing polo, I think I could double my wealth! However, in polo we spend so much time, effort, and pain and deplete our assets instead of building up our assets. You will always be making a loss in polo, and when it comes to investing in horses, it is important to be sensible and know your spending limits, as it can be very easy to get carried away.

The polo world, like business, has its share of people who try to take advantage of patrons for financial gain. My sons have faced such attempts and learned to recognize and avoid scams—skills that serve them well in business too. As a business leader, I approach polo with the same principles: I'll apologize when others are right but stand firm when I know my position is correct. Whether in business or polo, you must show strength when you're right, or people will take advantage. Above all, respect must be earned in both arenas.

Sometimes when I play polo, because of my momentum in life and my belief in righteousness, when things don't go my way, I get frustrated.

I have programmed myself to always do things in the right way for patients and in business, and this has led to my success. In healthcare you can't cheat the system. But in polo and other industries, you see a lot of compromised values and things that are not done in an ethical way.

These days I don't mind if I win or lose, but I have been very competitive in the past. I am a go-getter in business, and this mindset and ego mean I have been known to argue with the polo umpire. I believe British polo umpiring is killing British polo and destroying the joys of the sport, and when players don't get protection from the umpire, it can be very dangerous and even fatal.

However, I don't want to be in this scenario anymore; I just want to build my karma and my legacy and play for pure enjoyment. Chevy once said to me, "Dad, polo is just a sport. Have fun and don't be so aggressive! You always want to win." So I have taken on board what my son said, and after more than three decades of playing polo, I am learning how to be a better loser and how to accept losing more graciously. Every time we lose, it's an opportunity to analyze where we strayed from the line of the ball and how we can stay more focused next time. In polo and in life, losses aren't failures—they're lessons that help us refine our approach.

One of the reasons that makes polo such a challenge for me is that in all my years of business and at school, I have always been a winner. With any business, I know how to make it a success. However, in polo, I sometimes question, "Why am I not successful?" The fact is, you can control a lot of factors in business, but there are a lot of elements in polo you can't control. There is no such thing as perfection in polo, so I just aim to have fun in each game. When playing with family and friends, if we win together, we laugh, and if we lose together, we laugh. And whether we win or lose, we will be back to play another day.

Polo as a Family Legacy

Polo is our family sport and main interest, as we all love playing it, and for me, a successful team is a happy team with everyone enjoying their polo. It is going for a family polo trip and coming last but being the happiest people there. No matter what has been said on the field during the game, we come off the field and forget what was said, and we move on from it. Polo should be about participation and having fun and cordiality with other teams and never feeling hatred or anger, because at the end of the day, it is only a game.

When you get to a higher level in polo, it gets very complicated. I have another book in mind, which will be specifically about polo, and there will be a lot of truths and insights into the polo world! But all the hassle is worth it, as polo is so fun, and I do it for the love of the sport and how it brings us together as a family. While there is no financial gain, we get the benefit of the enjoyment of playing, strengthening our family bond, and learning more about each other and our strengths and weaknesses. It is fascinating to watch family members playing polo together and seeing how innately they connect in a game. Winning or losing is not the most significant part for us, but we try our best to have a good match, and it is important for me to try to score a few goals each time I play.

My most memorable polo game ever was playing together with Chevy, Joevy, and Garvy, with Lovy as a reserve, at the Snow Polo in Saint Moritz as a fifteen-goal handicap team. We made history as the first all-family team with all amateur players. My favorite teammates to play with are my sons, as they are reliable, and they play with all their might. We have a great dynamism and energy together on the field. Some more of my favorite tournaments we have played in as a family team have been the Mongolia Polo Open and the Snow Polo tournament in Aspen. When playing as a family team, we either play as a father and three sons or a father and two sons and a daughter, sometimes with a professional, depending on the tournament handicap.

Polo is not only a hobby but also a great way to stay mentally and physically fit. When I am at home in Ipoh, I spend my weekends riding up to twenty horses for around fifteen minutes each. This helps me improve my fitness, riding skills, and understanding of the horses, which is essential for performing well in matches.

I work almost 365 days each year, and I often wake up and look at emails in the middle of the night, as I like to reply to emails as soon as I receive them. They say a lot of world leaders sleep only four or five hours a night, but working constantly, my mind is always on overdrive, and it is very hard to switch off. Playing polo helps clear my mind, because no matter what is going on in my business or my personal life, when I get onto the polo field to play, I have to focus on the game. I can't think about anything else for the time I'm on the field. It is the only time I am able to let go of everything else and put all my thoughts and energy into one activity, as polo requires your full concentration. But it does give me other organized chaos to face!

My family and I are also interested in other sports, including golf, badminton, and running marathons. We are all very fit and do a lot of exercise, and playing other ball sports helps improve our polo ability, as it makes us more accurate when hitting the ball. It also helps us read the game better. In high-goal polo, you have split seconds to make a decision, and if you make the wrong move, you could lose a goal to the other team.

I am going to start alternating between playing polo and golf, as I am pretty good at driving and putting, and the golf course is also a good place to do business. But in comparison to polo, golf isn't very adrenaline fueled. There is a reason for the saying that playing polo is like playing golf during an earthquake.

One of the biggest changes I have noticed in polo over the years is the increasing cost. High-goal polo now is all about money—limited funds means you can't buy the fastest and most agile horses, and these days it is horsepower that makes the difference. I now have horses stabled in three countries, and I am continuing to buy auction horses and have also done some breeding, as I like the rewarding element of seeing young horses progress. I have bought many high quality ponies from ten-goal players and in auctions, and I have also done embryo transfer and cloned. Everything I do, I do it properly and professionally, so when it comes to horses, my approach is the same.

However, there are very few people who can afford to spend so much money on buying horses to play high-goal polo, which is why the governing bodies for polo such as the Argentine Polo Association (AAP) are, not surprisingly, concerned that polo is attracting fewer big patrons.

I attended a meeting on this issue hosted by the AAP, and I presented a picture to them of the Palermo Open, on field number one, and I described a substantial piece of meat there surrounded by hyenas and alligators. I then presented another image, where there was less meat, and the pieces were smaller, and with more predators around it. Everyone was laughing, but I explained that this is why polo isn't growing.

My solution, which I proposed to the AAP, is that each stakeholder needs to know everyone's responsibility. To ensure people don't get frustrated, a verbal contract should be made between patron and player. Patrons must know their commitment to make timely payments of the amounts as agreed. The players must perform dutifully and not create confusion or complication and play at their best and not betray the patron. Polo clubs should set up the rules and obey the rules and not take sides.

Polo is a niche sport, but it never used to be so expensive. The cost of entering a medium- or high-goal tournament and paying for professional players now—never mind the horses—is astronomical. When I first started playing competitively, we used to spend much less per tournament in Europe, with my wife and children joining for a holiday, and we had a great time. I also played an eighteen-goal tournament in Malaysia, and I employed three professional players at an affordable rate.

Another change I have noticed in polo is that while the standard of polo—horsepower, skill, speed, equipment, and facilities—has all improved, it is also getting more dangerous. I have had a few occasions where young players have come flying toward me at top speed, and thankfully I have responsive horses, so I can control them to avoid a full collision. The game is now so fast because there are a lot of up-and-coming young players trying to prove themselves, and the horses are pushed to the absolute limit. Former ten-goal player Memo Gracida commented in a *Hurlingham Polo Magazine* article that the way the rules are now being interpreted means the line of the ball is not being respected in polo these days, and I agree.

One hundred percent Beh family members team photo on snow polo field—media coverage program under CNBC billionaire game in Saint Moritz, Switzerland

A Passport to the World

If I didn't play polo, I would probably invest more time and money in car racing and more travel. But as former UK Prime Minister Winston Churchill famously said, "No hour of life is lost that is spent in the saddle," and this could not be more true. Churchill also told a team of Oxford University polo players, "A polo handicap is your passport to the world," and playing polo is a wonderful way to meet like-minded people from various cultures and places. Polo takes me to every corner of the globe, and wherever I am, someone in polo will call me for help, and I will always pick up the phone and do what I can for them. I like to be able to help other people to play and enjoy polo.

Because of this, I have an idea for an online platform, which would involve the AAP, USPA, and the Hurlingham Polo Association. If you are traveling, you will be able to find polo anywhere in the world via this international group, whether you want to play chukkas or a weekend tournament, or if you need to hire horses. I want to create more links and meeting opportunities in polo so more players can find patrons, and patrons can find exciting opportunities to play.

While I will no longer be playing polo competitively, I am looking forward to continuing to play family chukkas and supporting the polo journey for the third generation of the Beh family. As I pass the mallet to the next generation, I hope they will follow the line of the ball, not only in polo but also in life—pursuing their passions with focus, integrity, and determination.

My polo legacy includes successfully grooming Lovy, Chevy, Joevy, and Garvy into world-class nonprofessional high-goal players. Together, we've achieved countless international victories and individual accolades, solidifying our place in the sport awards in Argentina,

America, the United Kingdom, China, Chile, Mongolia, France, Spain, Malaysia, and Europe.

Joevy won two MVP awards in Argentina—Potrillitos and Potrillos at age of eleven and fourteen in 2000 and 2003, respectively. He was the first non-Argentine to win the Indios Potrillos tournament after thirty-eight years of Argentine dominance.

Both Chevy and Joevy represented England's national polo school team, captained by Chevy, while they were studying at high school in England.

Both Chevy and Joevy won the American National Intercollegiate All-Star Award, and their names were up at the USPA Museum of Polo and Hall of Fame in Florida. Chevy was inducted once and Joevy twice. Both were captains of the University of Virginia polo team for many years.

All Beh family members played on field number one at Palermo, Buenos Aires, which is equivalent to playing on Centre Court at Wimbledon, UK.

First Asian family to win the Mongolian World Polo Championship

Chapter 9

THE UPS AND DOWNS OF RUNNING A BUSINESS

Running a successful business brings contentment and enables you to improve your life and the lives of those around you. However, ups and downs are all part and parcel of running a company, and that is what keeps life interesting. Otherwise, if everything is plain sailing, life becomes monotonous, and when your mind is not occupied with improving your company, this can lead to deviation toward negative influences and a lack of focus that can have a destructive impact on your business.

Lessons from Business Partnerships

Generally, I have never had many problems in my business, because I'm very hands on; I control everything with my management, and people know they can't take advantage of me. The only times I have ever had problems have been working with partners and sharing a business with joint investment. In my experience having ventures with partners results in poor returns on investment. When the project goes well, they can change their motives and start cheating you left, right, and center to get all the money for themselves.

Indeed, one of the biggest challenges I have faced is entering into partnerships with nonhealthcare businesses outside of BP Healthcare Group. Every partnership I've invested in has been very successful and turned into a huge multibillion market cap profitable company, but when companies get to this level, people often have hidden agendas, and they become greedy. I have experienced this a number of times, and the moral of the story is that if you want to have a business, you should do it yourself without partners.

Many people have done too much borrowing, which means they generally have financial problems, even if they look wealthy from the outside. I have trusted people too much in the past, because they gave me the initial impression they were successful and credible on the surface, but in reality it was all deception. When they are deep in debt, close to bankruptcy—like being in the black hole of Calcutta, where everyone is struggling for survival—they will try all sorts of illegal and unethical tricks to rescue them from financial collapse.

This is a problem I struggle to solve, because other companies' financial positions are out of my control. I can do my research, but the company may not be transparent. I have outlined a particularly bad experience where I invested in a partnership that was my idea, my money, and my vision, and the project itself turned out well, but the partners were not honest, and they made me look like the villain while they appeared like heroes in the public eye. Even though this was not true, I ended up losing my total investment and got zero return.

The cases went to court, as advised by the Companies Commission of Malaysia (a.k.a. SSM in Malaysia), to extradite the regulators taking quicker action. I ended up spending a lot of money fighting the entire corrupt judiciary system. I lost the case within minutes in the virtual court, and I was so distraught I cursed the defense lawyer who was a former federal judge. Within a short period afterward, he had passed away. Perhaps this was God showing justice for me. This was the court case where the partner had cheated and illegally transferred my share without me knowing about it until my auditor discovered it during his annual routine audit, and there had been no negotiation. It was a shock to find out the government authorities had allowed this to happen in plain sight.

This is why I recommend caution when considering business partnerships. Joint ventures can be risky, and it is often wiser to run a smaller business independently and maintain full control of your business, even if it means operating on a smaller scale. Independence allows for greater flexibility, making it a preferable option for many entrepreneurs.

I often bring this incident up to make my children carefully consider if a project or partnership is worth pursuing. Every bad experience I've been through means my children can learn from it. This has made them wiser, so when Chevy was interested in starting new business ventures with some other well-known families from China's Special Administrative Region of Macau; Malaysia; Indonesia; and Thailand, I warned him to be very cautious without having a controlling stake. He listened to me and chose to dissolve three of these ventures and took back our capital, but he entered into one of them, and unfortunately it didn't work out.

Sadly, it is very hard to trust people in business, and there are certain things you are better off keeping to yourself. If you trust someone and you don't have much to lose, that is fine—go ahead and take the risk. After all, you only lose in kind. However, if you have a lot to lose, you should think very carefully before trusting people. When you put your trust in someone else, you have to calculate how much damage you can afford.

There is a saying attributed to Honoré de Balzac: "Behind every great fortune lies a great crime." Unfortunately, while luck and efficiency may help initiate wealth, the system also tolerates collusion, making Balzac's statement a common occurrence in business.

On the flip side, those in business know how tough it is to manage and finance a group by yourself, and I rely on my suppliers and customers supporting me and trusting in me. Thank goodness the bank trusted me all those years ago at the start of 1981 and helped finance that first laboratory. I had very little at that time, so it was all through character financing and the bank's belief in me, and I am pleased that I have delivered on my word.

Maintaining Financial Stability

So far in my business life, since that first loan I took out for five years, and paid it back in less than two and a half, I have experienced tight cash flow in the past, but I have never been in the position where I have not been able to pay my periodic financial obligations. This is because all my stakeholders, such as bankers, suppliers, and my staff, all trusted me, and my vision and my business model work. BP Healthcare Group has remained on an upward trajectory, growing organically since it was founded. Not many people can say that about their business.

When a business has no debt, there is no baggage. From day one until today, I am very lucky and blessed that my company has always been profitable. The only difference has been how much profit I have made at different times, and in the early days, I had mortgages to pay, as I bought properties for my outlets. If you do not own the property and you rent buildings, you are always at the mercy of the landlord.

Expansion Challenges in the Healthcare Sector

The healthcare sector is highly regulated, as the Malaysian Ministry of Health has very high standards for safeguarding patients, so once you own a property, you must ensure that the building and all the equipment meet the required specification. It often takes months (if you are very lucky), or even years, to attain an operating license. It is time-consuming to acquire the license, because if you do not own the property you plan to use as a medical facility, each time you need to move to a new property, you must apply for a new license. I ensure I have bought the property first to reduce the burden of having to reapply and waste valuable time getting a new license every time. In hindsight this is a blessing in disguise, as I have now amassed a portfolio of properties nationwide that enhance the group assets. Our profit and excess cash are always deployed for expansion to scale up our services from primary to tertiary care.

It has always been important for me to work hard and think about how to keep increasing my revenue—particularly in the early days of BP Healthcare Group—so I could keep scaling and invest in buying more of my own property. But as an entrepreneur, I am also a strong believer that as well as growing your business, you must be watchful that you do not overborrow to the extent that a profitable business has borrowed so much money it can't meet its financial obligations.

Navigating Operating Expenses and Profitability

Upscaling from primary to secondary and tertiary healthcare facilities incurs huge operating expenses paying the doctors and specialists. But without them, your facilities cannot operate. So initially you start off with high-operating costs and not much income, and cash flow becomes affected. However, in these times, the group has to stand strong and be patient to try to push new services, so once the services become more established, they go from being cost centers to profit centers.

For any business you run nationally, you have to consider the size of the population, and we have quite a small population in Malaysia, with only around thirty-four million people. It can be challenging operating a large company in a small country, as there are always other competitors trying to take up more space.

I always tell my children, if I were born in America and I ran BP Healthcare Group there, with a population of over 333 million people, my sales would be around ten times more than they are here in Malaysia. American lab tests are also eight times more expensive than in Malaysia, so if I were based in America, I would probably be on the Forbes list.

But by offering more services to our patients in Malaysia, we can generate more revenue. Primary care only has limited services, as do secondary and tertiary care. However, if we provide services in primary, secondary, and tertiary care, we are covering all the services a patient needs, and they might come to us ten times for ten different services, so I have the economy of scale in terms of purchase. What's more, my staff can multitask between primary, secondary, and tertiary care, so all my staff are highly productive, and I am very competitive, as I can defy the expensive operating costs of doctors and specialists. Crucially, it makes life easier for patients to be able to come to us as a one-stop center for all the services they need and not have to shop around.

The Impact of Economic Regulatory Factors

Since I was born until today, the economy in Malaysia has been generally stable. I have been lucky that if there have been dips in the economy, my business has kept going up. For example during COVID-19, we rose to the challenge to render services for the public.

I also had to be aware of the dynamic environment and the external influences and global trends that could affect my business. That is why we have taken a holistic approach and diversified our business to be a hypermarket in healthcare. But despite having a large market share, there are still many tricky external factors to navigate.

Of course, economic factors can cause changes to prices and the way we do things, and we often have to respond to ebbs and flows in the economy by modifying how we sell our products and services, such as adjusting prices or doing some more promotions to keep consolidating the public perception of our brand or to maintain or increase our sales.

However, local trends specific to people in Malaysia are often influenced by government requirements, so you have to be prepared for these changes as well. Some of the biggest problems we come across in the healthcare industry are regulatory requirements that can catch us out. The government can make it tricky sometimes, as governmental factors are always there, and when we want to expand, on average it takes between six and nine months to get government approval for the opening of a new outlet. Luckily we are a group that can support new outlets, but for individuals to come in who don't have existing business to start off with, they can put in all the capital and manpower, only to find the business is a nonstarter, so they have to reactivate again.

Ever since the government introduced accreditation in 1997, we were one of the first healthcare companies to seek and gain this accreditation. As well as being a stamp of approval from the government, it is also a way of safeguarding your business, because if you make a mistake or anything goes wrong, you can show that you have tried to follow procedure and do things properly by following government regulation.

There are also internal influences to consider, such as how you run a company and your profit and loss. If your company is losing money, you have to prepare yourself for a tussle to get back on track. Running a business is like fighting a battle every day. But there are things you can do to give yourself the best chance to run your business as smoothly as possible. I run my company with complete autonomy supported by a very competent management team to keep things as simple and streamlined as possible.

I would like to leave you with some key advice and words of wisdom I have learned from over forty-five years in business.

1. Check if there is demographic demand.

If I had to give one piece of advice about making money to the younger generation, I would say everyone wants to make money, so before you want to make money, you must first ask yourself truthfully if the product or service you want to sell is usable and salable. The first thing to do before starting any venture is to assess if there is a demand or need for the product or service. Do you like it, and will other people like it? You must get feedback from your target customer by doing market research, customer research, and research into future trends to assess what the current and future customer needs. To know who your target customer is, you must do a demographic study before you start doing business. Only then will it be clearer and more accessible for you to reach your goals. After ticking the boxes of all the above, you must ensure your product or service is affordable.

For example, SpaceX is an incredible opportunity to travel into space, but is it affordable?

2. Follow the Boy Scouts' motto: "Be Prepared."

I still approach business like a Boy Scout. To run a company, you must always be well prepared for whatever you are undertaking. Being in the Scouts teaches you to do good things to help others, have a good work ethic, show respect and honesty to others, and try to help other people to do well and bring out the best in them. It also teaches you how to be independent, how to improvise and problem-solve, and how to live at one with nature. These principles are particularly important in healthcare, but they will help any business run more successfully.

3. Secure God's blessing.

Despite all the effort you put in, God must bless you, and if you do not have God's blessing, you will fail. You get God's blessing by doing good things in life, as in the Boy Scouts, where we had to do at least one good deed every day to serve others. When you are blessed, your life and business will run more smoothly, as you will have inner happiness. Given our inability to directly contact God, we must present our requests in a simple, straightforward manner to increase our chances of being heard. There are so many devils around you trying to make you fail in business, but there is only one God. Challenges such as product misalignment, poor timing, insufficient funding, inadequate manpower, or restrictive regulations can hinder business success. How are you going to bypass the devils and secure God's assistance? You must help yourself first by working very hard and devote your time, intelligence, and knowledge to a product where there is a market and for which you have a clear objective. Even with divine guidance, a product or service that lacks market demand is unlikely to succeed.

4. Work hard and stay passionate.

Pursue your work with full commitment and passion. If you start a business and become successful with a good service or product, do not be content and think you are set for the future. This is when you will get bored and your sales will go stagnant. Whatever you achieve, aspire to work even harder and make your business even greater. You should continue to keep fighting and be a go-getter to keep progressing yourself and your company. We feel lost when we don't have a focus and a purpose.

If you are passionate and hardworking, this will filter down to your staff. You can't expect your staff to work overtime if you yourself are not putting in the hours as well. I start working as soon as I wake up in the morning, and I am still working when I go to bed at night. Having a motivated workforce is important, so you must love your staff so they genuinely want to work hard, achieve results, and share the success with you.

5. Keep it simple.

Clear communication is essential for avoiding confusion and ensuring staff, providers, and users understand expectations. Simple objectives and user-friendly interfaces help build trust and confidence.

To attract and retain customers, products and services must be user-friendly. Understanding your target audience, their needs, and behaviors is crucial. Design products with simplicity and clarity in mind, focusing on solving problems and providing value. Continuously gather user feedback and adapt to market trends to ensure your offerings remain relevant and effective.

Our BP Healthcare Group experience is designed to be user-friendly: log in online, arrive at the clinic with a barcode, use a self-service machine to print test stickers, complete the quick test, and receive results via email while driving home. This eliminates the risk of contamination and provides a fast, efficient process.

6. Be an expert in your industry.

I am a trained medical microbiologist, and my expertise as a specialist in this area helped me stand out from others at the start of my career. It is vital to study your area and become a fountain of knowledge before you start doing business. This will give you credentials and credibility. Never stop being hungry for learning. I have four degrees in total—a bachelor's degree in science from the University of Santo Tomas in the Philippines, a master of business administration from the Golden Gate University in the United States, a post-graduate diploma in medical microbiology with an ASEAN Science and Technology Fellowship from the Institute for Medical Research in Malaysia, and an honorary PhD in law at Nottingham University. Law is always a useful degree to have, no matter what industry you are in. Even now, as a medical microbiologist, I am a medical detective, and I can tell my doctors what the problem and cause are and how to give the right treatment.

7. Ensure value for money.

Offer discounts whenever possible to ensure patients receive affordable care. Patient health is paramount, and I never turn anyone away because of financial limitations. Providing quality healthcare to all is deeply rewarding, and I'm grateful for my patients' trust.

Reducing costs means you can pass the benefit on to your customers. For example, when I buy multiple machines, suppliers will give me a discount. A hospital may be able to buy one CT scanner, whereas I may buy ten and ask for more of a trade discount, as I have more centers to install them in. The more discounts I get on machinery, the less I need to charge customers for services. If I get a discount, I can give patients a discount, so there is a double discount, and it is a win-win situation. Furthermore, from the consumers' perspective, the more they buy, the more discount they get. If they buy packages for five to ten years, they will lock in their price and hedge inflation, paying the same price for the duration of their contract, plus I offer installment plans for customers who are unable to pay up front.

8. Align your actions with your values, not solely with monetary rewards.

When you are working in the healthcare sector, making money should be secondary to improving your services to help your patients. You should not be focused on the money you can make from it. Solve the patient's problem first, then think about the money. If they can pay, they will pay. If not, they will receive the treatment for free. This comes back to Joe Girard's law of 250 and the importance of looking after one client. One dissatisfied client could influence 250 people against using your product or service, whereas one happy customer could encourage 250 people to use your product or service.

Money will come to you if you do things properly and with integrity, have other people's best interests at heart, and offer products and services that genuinely help people and make their lives better in some way. When I first started BP Healthcare Group and began to build it up, I never thought of money when I was pursuing my dreams, but through hard work, perseverance, and passion, I have accrued a lot of wealth while also improving the lives of others.

9. Embrace new approaches and find innovative solutions—think outside the box.

My advice to everyone, particularly graduates, is not to be too restricted or overdependent on your training or the degree you achieve. Be adaptable and flexible to market requirements. You can be successful in many ways; your degree is just a passport that demonstrates you are educated and capable, so companies see you with a degree, and they think they can train you up. It is okay for your training and perspective at work to be different from others, as your unique ideas can add value to your job or business. Never shy away from sharing your ideas, no matter how far out of the box they seem. For those studying at university, I want to advocate for people to make a difference and differentiate themselves from the market. Rather than looking for a job, I aim to inspire people to be entrepreneurs and be their own bosses and help create employment. Make yourself an asset to the country by providing jobs rather than looking for jobs.

10. Remember that success requires dedication and perseverance.

We are living in a world of instant gratification, where people aspire to get rich quick by only putting in the minimum amount of time and effort. While playing with shares and cryptocurrency such as Bitcoin may facilitate a quick accumulation of wealth, it is also a very risky game of luck, and most of the time, you lose. Even if you do get lucky, nobody who tries to make money in this way will achieve long-term gains and financial stability. In the end they go bankrupt. Entrepreneurial success is not a quick dash; it is a grueling marathon. If you are not prepared to work hard and be in it for the long run, weathering the highs and lows and learning lessons along the way, you will not reach the destination you are aiming for. It might sound cliché, but Rome wasn't built in a day. My own business journey of over forty-five years and still counting shows how hard work really does pay off over time.

Malaysia versus France test match

Conclusion

Some people who read this book may already know me and have even met me, in which case they may already be familiar with some of my story. But very few people know how my background has shaped the businessman and father I am today. Through this book I want to share my true journey from childhood to the present day, as well as some of my thoughts on the future. I also hope to create awareness of BP Healthcare Group's positive impact on the lives of millions of people in Malaysia.

The underlying message of this book is that if you respect the line of the ball by doing things in the right way and being a caring, genuine person, you will bring good karma to your life and your business. As a Buddhist, I believe my family and ancestors must have done a lot of good things in their lives to bless me, and I, too, want to continue these blessings for my future generations. I am creating credit for future generations of my family, comparable to accruing airline points that can be transferred or used for discounts on flights. You can redeem karma for your own consumption, which your ancestors laid the foundations for, but you must also continue to keep building it yourself so those after you will benefit.

I respect everyone to reciprocate respect from them, and the first lesson I taught my children is to love everyone, be generous to everyone, and mean no one any harm, whatever you do in life. It may seem simple, but many people fail because of the fundamental flaw that they are not pleasant and helpful to others.

In some ways life can be looked at like a snakes and ladders board game—the older generation will know this board game; the younger generation may not. When you land on a ladder, you move up the board, and if you land on a snake, you move down the board. There is no real strategy or intelligence to success in snakes and ladders; it is all based on the roll of the dice and how much perseverance and tenacity you have to make the best of whatever you are dealt.

Some people will reach their destinations faster than others, as the ups and downs are mostly out of your control. But when you go backward rather than forward, you should never give up. Snakes are temporary setbacks, and you've got to hang on and keep looking for the next ladder to help you climb back up to the top. Do not drop off the board and give up. I would never consider myself as smarter than anyone else, but I am blessed with more ladders in my life than snakes, because I am always looking onward and upward, even if I have to take a step back every now and then.

To be a successful entrepreneur, you don't need anyone to teach you; it is already in you to be an independent thinker and a game changer in your industry. You must be creative and unique in your products and services and be prepared for enormous challenges along the way, with more steps back than steps forward at times, and a lot of mental, physical, and financial pressure. But the most important thing is to maintain passion and perseverance.

There are millions of reasons to fail, but you must be passionate about relentlessly pursuing your purpose. With true dedication and devotion, you will see no barriers to achieving your goals. Don't get confused about what your target is or get distracted along the way; just keep moving forward and never give up.

This is a saying I live by: "Winners never quit, and quitters never win."

In business, it is important to keep moving forward before others catch up with you and to make sure you move far enough ahead so that you are the only one in the running and you can control the market. Just as in polo, you must push to be first to the line of the ball so you get the first opportunity to hit the ball and score the winning goal.

Looking to the future, there is a lot of disruption and innovation happening in the healthcare industry. A culture I have tried to foster in my children and my staff is to always be very agile, adapt quickly, and be movers and shakers. BP Healthcare Group will be the first to adopt any new innovations in Malaysia. I had the foresight to see how my initial pathology lab could grow and diversify into a plethora of different areas of the healthcare business, so now, if our main BP Healthcare Group business is disrupted, we have many other businesses in our group, from waste management to selling IT systems, and we are currently expanding into a veterinary care business.

We are living in uncertain times, but as long as my children and the next generation continue to be hungry for success, stay humble, and have the same drive, fire, motivation, discipline, and persistence as I have, if not more, they will be able to adapt the BP Healthcare Group to any circumstances, even during another pandemic.

As I reflect on my journey, it brings me a lot of happiness that the state of Perak is enjoying all the fruits of my creation. Likewise, across Malaysia, people now have access to superlative health services provided by BP Healthcare Group right at their doorstep. I feel as if I have moved the mountain to Muhammad.

By telling my story, I hope to inspire you that your hopes and aspirations can turn into reality if you are willing to persevere. I also want to set an example that even from humble beginnings and limited resources, through hard work, determination, and following the line of the ball, you can build the life of your dreams while helping others improve their lives along the way.

[to refer to BP Healthcare Group POLO Facebook(@bppolo) for more photos]

About the Author

Dr. Beh Chun Chuan is the founder and chairman of BP Healthcare Group, one of Malaysia's largest healthcare organizations. Starting with a single pathology lab in 1981, he has built BP Healthcare Group into a comprehensive healthcare provider with over 120 outlets nationwide. A devoted father to Lovy, the late Chevy, Joevy, and Garvy, Dr. Beh is also an avid polo player who has competed internationally at the highest levels, including matches at the prestigious Palermo grounds in Argentina.